Take Care of your music Business

Second Edition

PJ KELLY & Associates

TAKE CARE OF YOUR MUSIC BUSINESS

Second Edition

Taking the Legal and Business Aspects You Need to Know to 3.0

JOHN P. KELLOGG, ESQ.
FOREWORD BY ISAAC SLADE

PJ's Publishing
A Division of PJ KELLY & Associates
Massachusetts

Copyright © 2014 by PJ KELLY & Associates, Malden, Massachusetts 02148.

Published by PJ's Publishing, a division of PJ KELLY & Associates, Malden, Massachusetts 02148.

All rights reserved, including the right of reproduction in whole or in part in any form.

Library of Congress Cataloging-in-Publication Data

Kellogg, John P.
Take care of your music business/John P. Kellogg
Includes index.
ISBN: 978-0-9675873-3-2

Title: Take Care of Your Music Business, Second Edition

Cover design: Laurence J. Nozik, www.geminisd.com
Photo credits: front cover Mychal Lilly, foreword, Frank Ockenfels

First edition, copyright 2000, PJ KELLY & Associates
Reprint, one
Second edition, First paperback edition, copyright January 2014
First paperback printing
Manufactured in the United States of America

This book is intended to increase awareness of the legal and business aspects within the music industry. The author will not be held responsible or liable for any information in this book that is used independently by any person or company. While this book was written to render the solid information contained herein, it is not to be considered a substitute for legal and professional advice of any kind and is not provided with that intent. No part of this book may be used for any purpose without the prior written consent of the publisher and the author. Contact the publisher at pjpublishing01@gmail.com.

CONTENTS

Acknowledgements　　xi

Foreword　　xiii

1 **Growth and Development of the Music Industry**　　1

2 **What is a Music Production Company?**　　8

3 **The Three Big P's**　　10
   Still the Keys to Success in Today's New Music Industry

4 **Choosing the Proper Business Structure for Your Production Company**　　18
   Sole Proprietorship
   General Partnership
   Corporation
   Limited Liability Company (LLC)

5 **The Across the Board Deal**　　26
   How to Maximize Income for Your Production Company

6 **The New Business Model**　　31
   A Look at the 360° Deal—Labels and More Venture "Across the Board"

7 Contracts and Accounting Statements 36
Introduction

8 Exclusive Recording Artist Contract 38
Analysis of Artist/Production Company 360° Agreement

9 Statement and Analysis of Recording Earnings 95
Why having a Million-Seller doesn't Mean a Million Dollar$ to the Artist

10 Copyright Principles 107
The Copyright "Bundle of Rights"

11 Exclusive Songwriter Contract 117
Analysis of Songwriter/Publishing Company Agreement

12 Co-Publishing and Administration Contract 145
Breakdown of Co-Publisher/Publisher Agreement

13 Statement and Analysis of Copyright Earnings 162
How the Copyright Money Flows

14 Personal Management Contract 170
A Preview

15 Statement and Analysis of Management Earnings 200
Maximizing the Earnings of the Artist

16 The Live Performance	**204**
Having It, Working It, Making It	
17 The Evolving Digital Age	**210**
From the Ground to the Cloud	
18 Incorporating the Information	**214**
19 Moving You and Your Business into the Future	**216**
Index	233
Bio	243

To my Lord and Savior, Jesus Christ, I give thanks for the continued health, strength, and opportunity to spread knowledge and share my talents in beneficial ways.

I dedicate this book to my wife Sandra, my children, family, and the memory of my wonderful parents, the late Ruth W. and Attorney John W. Kellogg.

ACKNOWLEDGMENTS

A thank you is in order to the many business associates and clients I've had the opportunity to work with, and for, through the years. Without the interactions, sharing, and challenges, fewer lessons would have been taught or learned, my scope would not be as broad, and my experiences would not be as embellished. I extend my gratitude to Berklee College of Music, where I am honored to serve as Assistant Chair of the Music Business/Management department, for the opportunity to gain valuable experience as both an educator and administrator. Also, I'd like to recognize and thank the Black Entertainment and Sports Lawyers Association (BESLA), an organization dedicated to the mentoring and development of talent soon to be introduced to the sports and entertainment world, for their support of my endeavors throughout the years and to Music and Entertainment Industry Educators Association (MEIEA) members across the country who educate the next generation of leaders of the entertainment industry.

FOREWORD

It's what we do.

Whether it's a song, or a connection, or just a transaction, I prize the focus and direction it takes to know what I want. With people I work with, I'm looking for folks who have vision, who know where they're headed and who understand what's going on today as well as what's coming down the line.

Back in the day, when we were just getting started, my band was just playing songs to each other in my basement just outside of Denver. I remember thinking it would be so much easier to stay there, practicing after class, keeping our day jobs, never really risking or putting ourselves out there—at least it was a guarantee of never getting rejected. Eventually, we started thinking it might be worth taking a crack at writing some songs and playing around town. I was finishing up my degree at University of Colorado at Denver, and I needed a professor to sponsor an independent study for one of my final credits. As I looked for a faculty advisor, Professor Kellogg's name kept coming up, so I scheduled an interview and I asked John if he would be my faculty advisor. I told him about a TV show concept I wanted to try about the local music scene called Noise Floor. I'd heard about his great classroom delivery and was familiar with some of his life long clients. I also knew I had to have it together to prove to him I was ready and able to take the concept to pilot and get it aired. I went to his office (he says "burst in") and gave him my pitch and he agreed to sponsor me. I even somehow managed to convince him to let me interview him as well. The next day I went to John's office armed with lights, camera & film crew (really just me) to interview him. He was gracious to say the least.

Soon after, a local channel picked up my show and we started getting some episodes off the ground. John was right there, working on the legal and business development of Noise Floor with me. As the TV show was starting to pick up speed, our band was emerging from the basement and starting to play some shows around town in Denver. Over the course of two years, he counseled and guided me through the process of business development of the show, as well as toss in some much needed advice about running a band, even after the project was done and I graduated. I was really impressed with his music industry connections and how he immediately plugged me in to some New York contacts he thought would be beneficial to me, all while working hand-in-hand with my own attorney to protect my business interests as my band started making some headway.

I remember as we first started talking to labels, our drummer, Ben Wysocki, was enrolled in one of John's music business classes and he'd pick on Ben as often as he could. "What'd they tell you yesterday, Ben? Think you'll go for it? Tell us how that one deal's looking." We've been able to keep up over the years, and I'm told he still uses our band as a test case in some of his intro to music classes. I'm really glad we've been able to stay in touch over the years. He shoots straight and has that rare mix of knowledge *and* experience. Most folks out there have an abundance of one or the other. He's been such an encouragement to me as our band has navigated our own ups and downs with the ever-changing music industry since we started playing professionally back in 2004. I can hear it in his voice whenever we catch up. He's seen too many people rise and fall in this business and he's reminded me to take care of myself, enjoy the little things, soak it all up, memorialize the moment. He's been a source of knowledge and encouragement since the beginning of my career.

John brought something special to UCD with his book, his writings, his background in the business, his teaching style and the determination to set his students up for the real world. I know 3.0

reflects his insatiable quest to keep the players in the music business thriving.

I'm glad you're holding the Second Edition of Take Care of Your Music Business. It's a really informative and up-to-date manual on what you need to know to make a living playing music, while also making sure to cover your bases and not get taken. It's also proof that John & I, and people like us are still taking ideas, focusing and developing them, and sharing them with the world. In the music business, it's a risk to put yourself out there, but it's what you've got to do. Otherwise you're just playing music in your basement.

Isaac Slade

Isaac Slade, recording artist and CEO is the lead singer of The Fray. Isaac formed the group in 2002 with guitarist and vocalist, Joe King. Now, along with Dave Welsh on guitar and Ben Wysocki on drums, The Fray can be heard on television, radio, and seen live in concert from their hometown Denver to most anywhere around the world. Check their tour schedule at www.thefray.com.

(Left, The Fray's Joe King, Dave Welsh, Isaac Slade and Ben Wysocki.) Photo credit, Frank Ockenfels

1

Growth and Development of the Music Industry

The music business is a dynamic intersection of art and commerce that is and always has been, shaped by technological innovation and entrepreneurship. While we are in fact currently in the midst of a paradigm shift from consuming music in various forms of physical to digital configurations, the accompanying rumors of the music industry being dead or dying are greatly exaggerated. It is true that since the beginning of the 21st century, the recorded music industry has undergone significant downsizing on all levels, but other areas of the music industry are growing. Some music pundits and savvy investors envision a revival of recorded music revenues based on music subscription services, ad-supported streaming and other new business models.

A person prophesying the end of the music business is not a new phenomenon. Over the last 120 years of the music business as we know it, there have been several times when new technology has caused a disruption in the progress of the business of music making, and each time, there have been predictions of imminent disaster. Astronomer and author, the late Dr. Carl Sagan once noted, "You have to know the past to understand the present."

In the early 1900s, entrepreneur Louis Shapiro started the business that would become the, still active, publishing company, Shapiro & Bernstein. At that time, sheet music was the second-leading music industry revenue stream after live performance. When piano-roll makers refused to pay publishers any royalties for using compositions on these first mechanical reproductions of music publishers sought, but were denied, relief in the courts. Concerned that this invention may end the business as they knew it, the publishers lobbied Congress and had the copyright law amended requiring the payment of a mechanical royalty for each use of songs on piano-rolls and, to their pleasant surprise, both the sheet music and piano-roll business flourished. When entrepreneurs like Harry Pace started Harlem-based Black Swan Records and sold popular Blues recordings in great numbers, publishers were again concerned that no one would buy sheet music if they could buy recordings of the songs and play them at home.

Although publishers received mechanical royalties for such sales, they were legitimately concerned the sheet music business would falter. Didn't happen! Both businesses grew larger. When radio started programming music on a regular basis during the Great Depression in the latter 20s and early 30s, it initially brought live performance, sheet music and recordings sales to its knees. Publishers and record companies feared the public would never again want to pay for sheet music and records when they could hear the music for free on the radio. What happened? Growth. Even though records couldn't be made in great numbers during WWII, the market for American music grew substantially as a result of the Armed Forces Radio Network of over 90 radio stations that broadcasted the great array of American repertoire and artists worldwide.

After the war, sales of instruments, records, record players and sheet music exploded, all while musician-entrepreneurs Duke Ellington, Harry James, Louis Armstrong, Frank Sinatra, Billie Holiday and Louis Jordan led bands that performed all over the world.

Contemporary music education had its beginnings in the 1940s, when musician and entrepreneur, Lawrence Berk, recognized World War II veterans wanted to pick up an instrument and play like their big-band heroes, whose music had inspired them during the dark days of war. Berk decided to fill a void left by music conservatories that taught only classical music and wanted nothing to do with teaching budding musicians the popular music of the day. In addition to the desire to play, these veterans had a source of financing for their education, the G.I. bill, which insured Berk could be paid for his services. To that end, he opened the Schillinger House in Boston in 1945, a school that specialized in teaching the Schillinger method of arranging contemporary music. In the early fifties it evolved into the Berklee College of Music.

The midpoint of the 20th century also ushered in further technological innovation, entrepreneurial pursuits and cultural changes that significantly advanced the development of the music and entertainment industry. Television was a new technological development that instantly expanded the mass media landscape and several weekly radio dramatic serial programs and personalities migrated to it, leaving a void in radio programming that reduced the value of radio properties and opened doors for new owners eager to expand the rigid programming formats of radio. Many of them chose to program a new form of music—an amalgamation of Blues (Jump Blues), Gospel, Jazz and Pop—called Rhythm and Blues (R&B). Young entrepreneurs like New York's Ahmet Ertegun of Atlantic Records, Chicagoan Leonard Chess's Chess Records, Vivian Carter and James Bracken's Veejay Records of Gary, Indiana and Art Rupe's Los Angeles based Specialty Records took the risk of recording and distributing this new wave of music and, by doing so, laid the foundation of Rock and Roll.

Several technological advancements including the development of stereophonic sound recording and reproduction; new configurations of recorded product the album and 45 RPM singles; the saturation of jukeboxes in both drinking and eating establishments; and the development and growth of the transistor radio market combined with the cultural shift of baby-boomers consuming R&B and Rock and Roll music increased the annual revenue generated from the sale of records from approximately $200 M in 1954 to over $600M in 1958.

The time was hot and changes came quickly. This rapid growth also ignited the entrepreneurial passion in a new wave of creative talents, including hit recording artists like Sam Cooke, Ray Charles and Frank Sinatra, who demanded and received ownership of their recording and publishing works. Another eager songwriter turned businessman, Berry Gordy, also risked a family loan of $800 to start Motown Records in 1958. And Europe wasn't lost on the movement. There was the onslaught of American Blues, R&B and Rock & Roll in Europe and it inspired a host of English musicians to develop a new genre of music that infiltrated the sixties and seventies: Rock.

Consumers were gaining more freedom to compile their own playlists of songs to play in their homes and automobiles in the 70s as Cassette tape and 8-track technology grew while the recording industry experienced growth simultaneously as album sales rivaled the sale of singles as the predominant sales configuration of music. Corporations, like Columbia Records, recognized the low-cost/high return potential of record companies and invested in purchasing independent labels or developing sub-labels that specialized in niche markets like R&B and Disco. The rise of Disco music, spurred on in the late 70s by the cross-promotion of films like "Saturday Night Fever" and "Thank God It's Friday" took record sales to another high point. But by the early eighties, after a public backlash against Disco, rise in sales of video games and piracy there was rapid decline in record sales. Once again, naysayers predicted the death of the record business. New technological innovation would soon intervene.

The SONY Walkman debuted in 1980 and was the first portable personal cassette player that revolutionized the way people consumed music followed by the compact disc technology, promising consumers an indestructible product and superior digital sound quality previously lacking in analog configurations. A new cable TV network, MTV, introduced the public to music videos that created a new promotional tool for record companies and heightened the public's interest in purchasing records of new talents. Michael Jackson's "Thriller" ushered in the era of long-form videos and Prince's feature film, "Purple Rain" heightened the demand for albums in the CD format.

Major labels, RCA, Polygram, MCA, WEA and Columbia continued to acquire or develop independent and sub-labels in the 80's as CD sales, and resulting profits started to soar. In the 90s many of these labels began to consolidate and increase their influence through a tremendous uptick in profits as many consumers replaced their vinyl or cassette collections with CD versions of the same music and CD sales started to eclipse cassettes and vinyl albums as the predominant configuration of music and earnings of these conglomerates reached record peaks. In an effort to expand their income, the major labels discontinued the sale of singles, forcing consumers to buy an entire CD album. However, this tactic led to growing discontent with the buying public, who resented having to purchase an entire CD in order to own the one or two singles they actually desired. But, the same digital technology used to develop the CD twenty years earlier and led to an epic comeback of the record industry in the 80s and 90s also set the stage for the perfect storm to come.

In the mid-nineties the development of MP-3 technology enabled audio recordings to be compressed in a digital format that allowed for Internet sharing. Napster mastered the peer-to-peer file sharing process and enabled the public to freely share audio recordings. The growth of this site quickly and drastically affected the sale of physical records. Major labels were slow to respond but eventually decided to attack this problem on two fronts: 1) suing P2P file sharing sites like Napster, and; 2) suing individual users of P2P technology (i.e., their potential customers). The second effort was met with anger and backlash from the public and damaged the labels' own efforts at starting online music store models like SONY and Universal Music's Pressplay and its rival Musicnet. Record company earnings from recordings peaked at $14B in 1999 and suffered double-digit declines in several of the following years, going down to $6.4B in 2012. However, technology was turning to enable music to regain its footing.

In 2003 there was a glimmer of hope in the works to change this dour situation when Steve Jobs of Apple computer fame devised a new model of digital music distribution and sales—iTunes—that revolutionized the music industry. iTunes was an immediate success, offering the sale of singles for $.99 (similar to the $1.00 price tag of singles in the 60's) and albums for $9.99. Apple's introduction of digital media players, iPod, iShuffle and later, the iPhone, led to its domination of the digital music sales market before the end of the first decade of the 21st century. Several other technological achievements in the Internet space during this decade, including satellite radio, Internet streaming services such as Pandora, Rhapsody, Muve, advanced the theory espoused by David Bowie and others at the beginning of the new millennium that someday music "will flow like water" and people will pay for unlimited access to music rather than purchasing and owning CDs. Development was changing course—and music continued to grow.

Tech gurus argued that strict adherence to copyright laws interfered with their ability to innovate and construct a new digital marketplace for music. Over a course of years, a combination of music label licensing agreements and governmental regulations allowed new technical advancements like YouTube, Spotify and others to offer services that combine free, ad-supported streaming and unlimited subscription service access to millions of songs and videos. While songwriters, artists and labels have reservations about the reduced royalty rates they provided these upstart services, the hope is that as the services' customer bases and revenues expand in the coming years, the royalty rates will be adjusted upward to fairly compensate the creators and record companies that provide these important services and products.

Several entrepreneurs including Sonicbid's Panos Panay and CD Baby's Derek Sivers created Web sites that empowered both musicians and their customers with valuable ancillary services and products that advanced the development of the new digital age in music. TuneCore, Myspace, Topspin, Facebook, Twitter, Kickstarter, PledgeMusic and other sites created digital distribution, direct-to-consumer retail and marketing services, social networking and crowd funding opportunities for artists and labels alike. Now, individual artists have the ability to create audio and video recordings and exploit them on YouTube, Soundcloud and other Internet sites and if an artist's video of a cover recording gets several hundred thousand views on YouTube, a significant number of Facebook likes and other indications of viral trending success within a few days of posting, a major label may decide to offer them a contract. As a matter of fact, most labels are more inclined to sign artists that have proven success in attracting and maintaining an audience through social networking.

So why would an artist desire to contract with a major label if they are already selling their own product on the Internet when they are already both a production company and a label selling audio recordings online through sites like iTunes and Amazon? To take advantage of the major label's vast network of physical distribution outlets, greater marketing and promotion opportunities and, well, just the prestige of saying you've got a major label contract is the usual response to this question…and there is some validity to these claims, even as now, more than ever, artists have the opportunity to run their own production company and label. Either way, whether you continue as an entrepreneur with your own production company/label or sign with a major, to grow and development, it is imperative that you handle your business properly and take care of your music business.

2

What is a Music Production Company?

A music production company is a business that is in charge of, or responsible for, the production and delivery of master recordings of songs ready for manufacture and commercial release. A production company may consist of one or more individuals doing business together in a room inside a home, an office building, or someone's basement or garage. It may or may not have a recording studio.

Many times, music production companies are like "subcontractors" to the major record label and the major label may rely on the production company to not only locate and discover new artists, but also to nurture and groom these artists' talents.

This is a big change from the way the record companies were run over fifty years ago, when the labels had staff A&R representatives whose primary job was to find new talent to develop. At the time, the label would absorb the business overhead expenses of maintaining an office, a recording studio, and a staff of in-house songwriters or producers to develop and direct the recording of the artists in a manner, which would create a distinctive style and sound (i.e., Motown Sound, Stax Sound, Sound of Philadelphia).

The label would also pay for its lawyers to handle the in-house agreements between staff producers, songwriters, and artists while their accountants would account to the various parties.

As time went on, rock and R&B music became dominant genres. Due to the frequent change of the popular sound and artists who were often singer-songwriters who now wanted to produce their own music, the labels were not as capable of successfully developing hit artists on an in-house basis. Spurned by necessity, they saw an opportunity to reduce their business overhead expenses and still get the product needed to compete in the market. This was achieved by contracting with the artists' production companies or independent production companies who discovered and produced new talent on an act-by-act basis. Not only did this make the labels more adept at handling the rapid changes in the marketplace, but it also eliminated the need to pay for the handling of the day-to-day business of contracting and monitoring the activities of producers, songwriters, and artists, which had now shifted to the production companies.

These new production companies, some of which were headed by former label staff employees, were now fully independent businesses, saddled with the responsibility and expense of forming and staffing an entity, contracting with other producers, songwriters, and artists, and even negotiating and monitoring agreements with record labels for the release of their product.

It has now progressed to the point where there are literally thousands of music production companies. On one CD you might find as many production companies responsible for the CDs tracks as you do the number of tracks on the CD. In many cases self-produced artists will record a song and accompanying video for uploading to SoundCloud or YouTube and place the recording for sale on digital music outlets like iTunes, Amazon or others. In this case, the production company is also serving as its own label.

This massive growth in the number of music production companies has not only led to opportunities for the new business owners, but has also created a challenge for those businesses to adhere to sound business principles and practices in order to grow and succeed.

3

The Three Big P's
Still the Keys to Success in Today's New Music Industry

I've been known to say that show business is 10% show and 90% business. I applaud you for buying this book and being interested in understanding the 90% business part of the equation, because without that part, the show and the dough will not go on. Even though you know the music, or you know many of the musicians, or you know a lot of the A&R reps who work with talented songwriters, producers, and artists, it won't mean anything if you don't know the legal and business aspects. You may even get that "Viral Hit" but if your lawyer hasn't properly prepared contracts with your clients, artists, producers, and songwriters, you may not be able to continue the relationship so that you can benefit from the second, third, and fourth hits. If your accountant does not properly take care of your business so that you can receive the highest return on your investment in discovering, nurturing, and grooming the next Chris Brown, Justin Bieber, Taylor Swift, Big Sean or Tamela Mann, you will definitely not achieve that Cash Money/Young Money, Dr. Luke, Rick Rubin or Big Machine type of success you're looking for. If you, the songwriter, artist, or producer, have no understanding of the contract's terms and the effect of those terms on your earning capacity, you, too, might sell millions of singles, sell out concerts and merchandise, receive lucrative endorsement and sponsorship contracts, yet, end up with nothing.

So, rather than give you the hype and the puff about the parties and the possibility of becoming a millionaire overnight, I want the end result of your time spent reading this book to be the recognition, realization, and application of what I call the three big principles, or the Three Big P's for Success, in today's music industry.

After reading this book you will have gained an understanding of the last two Big P's, but the first Big P—*Powerful Product*—goes far beyond anything that can be stated or discussed in this or any other book. It's what comes from the heart and is laid in the tracks. And because of that, I will deal with this P first.

POWERFUL PRODUCT

I once heard George Daniels, owner of not just any retail record establishment, but the infamous George's Music Room in Chicago, Illinois, say that music is "memories and emotion."

And he was right. The job of a successful production company is to develop and produce **Powerful Product** that captures, in a song, emotions strong enough to cause memories to last forever. A piece of powerful product has to create with music emotions that are so strong that a remake of the record or song will evoke memories years after its first release. I recently heard two songs by R&B divas, Chrisette Michelle and Fantasia, that featured samples of hits by my former clients, The O'Jays and The Commodores that are examples of that principle. Michelle's song, "Couple of Forevers" used the musical refrain of The O'Jays 70's hit "Family Reunion" and Fantasia's "Lose to Win" featured portions of the Commodores 80's hit "Nightshift." Both songs reached the Top Ten of the R&B Songs chart in *Billboard* magazine and owe a debt of gratitude to the powerful product created by the prior generations of great artists. Powerful product is everywhere and its definition shouldn't be limited to recordings. These days powerful product may be a great song or live performance that engages an audience, an innovative Web site or app, even a brand, all of which are assets that grow in value over time.

Powerful product is everywhere. I checked in again with Sandra Jackson, author of soon to release, For the Heart of Your Soul: Sweet Tea and Hot Coffee, about "powerful product." She said: "It's still the best beat going that you'll turn to at any time, year after year. It's the lyric that captivates you in maybe one or two words or with a line embedded deep in the song that lifts you, almost empowers you. It's still Smokey's 'Oooh Baby, Baby;' and the Temptations eases a traffic jam in any city."

Memories and emotion drive this business. Selling memories and emotion is this business and **Powerful Product** is the engine which runs this business! Powerful product is hard to describe, but you know it when you see, hear, or 'feel' it and you will see, hear or 'feel' if for years to come.

PROPER PERSPECTIVE

There are two important components to gaining the **Proper Perspective** of doing business as a production company in today's music industry. One component is external and the other is internal. **Both are critical to the future of your business.** The *external factor*, over which you have no control, is to recognize that the successful record labels operate on a very sophisticated level and are out to maximize their value for the benefit of shareholders and the continued success of their business. Repeat that to yourself when you wonder if the record label is interested in making new friends or meeting their bottom line.

During one of the industry's peak years, 1998, the merger of major labels Universal/MCA with Polygram reduced what we, here in the U.S., used to refer to as the "Big 6" major labels to the "Big 5." Immediately following, each member of the Big 5 vertically integrated their record manufacturing and distribution operations, lowering their per unit cost while increasing and maintaining the actual retail selling price of CDs to above $11, drastically improving their bottom line.

Mergers and acquisitions of major labels continued in the new millennium. What was the Big 5 in the 90s has become the Big 3 currently, as SONY Music Entertainment, Universal Music Group and Warner Music Group are the sole remaining major labels that represent 80–90% of the U.S. record sales. While each major has both creative and A&R staffs, their main function is manufacturing, distribution and marketing of the vast array of recordings culled from their relationships with production company imprints, affiliated labels, sub-labels and distribution only deals with independent labels. So, whether you do business on your own or with the major record label, it is important to have the proper perspective about the major's business relationship with these primary providers of music.

The *internal component* is to understand that when major record labels advance money to music production companies, they are, in essence, funding the start (and hopefully the continuation) of a business which you *do* have control over. It is important to remember that money received for funding the business is not solely for the personal use of the production company owner. It is for defraying the many costs associated with the creation and production of recordings upon which the production company's business is based.

Developing the proper perspective will help you to appreciate money for what it actually is and to put into practice the strategies that should lead to more successful control of your funds. To help you better understand this, I would like to share a theory I have on "When a Million Dollars Ain't a Million Bucks."

There are a lot of people who are attracted to the music industry because of the potential to make "big money." This belief is certainly nurtured by the barrage of stories that appear daily in the news media about the millions of dollars made by a few artists, producers, and songwriters. What these stories usually fail to mention are the costs to operate their businesses. The operating costs are borne primarily by the artists, producers, and songwriters who receive those millions. To put this very essential point in perspective, I think it's important to know "When a Million Dollars Ain't a Million Bucks."

Many times you hear the term "a million bucks" in lottery commercials and, in that context, when we think of lottery winnings, we think of money given with "no strings attached." Everyone knows that the IRS always has its strings attached, even with lottery winnings, but, after that, most people know these "winnings" are free and clear of other strings. Well, a million dollars advanced by a major record label to a music production company has many strings attached (*including* the IRS!).

I told you before about my cousin, Clark Kellogg. He's currently a basketball color analyst for CBS, but he used to be an all-pro forward for the NBAs Indianapolis Pacers (he's on the "big side" of the family). He played in the early 1980s and it was reported in a newspaper at the time, that his yearly salary was $450,000, which is small in comparison to the $100 million multi-year contracts signed by some NBA stars today. After recovering from the fact that my little cousin was making that much money, I decided to calculate the amount of his biweekly check. After doing the calculation over a fifty-two-week year, I concluded that a $17,000 gross check every other week sounded like a pretty decent amount for someone to start building financial security. Even after satisfying Uncle Sam's attached string, a net of $12,000 to $13,000 every two weeks to spend, save, or invest on a personal level still sounded pretty good. And that caused me to think about the difference between salaries paid to athletes and "advances" made to music production companies. It's a comparison of what I call "a million dollars versus a million bucks" and brings up an interesting analogy that best illustrates my theory "When a Million Dollars Ain't a Million Bucks." I hope this analogy helps create the proper perspective of the "million-dollar contract" in the music industry.

Let's say there is an athlete (an NFL football player) and a music production company owner sitting in a bar comparing notes. The football player says, "Man, I just signed a million-dollar contract." The music company production owner, not to be outdone, says, "You too, man? I also just signed a million-dollar contract today." The question is, who has a "million dollars" and who has the "million bucks?"

The athlete makes the "million bucks" in that he has the almighty IRSs string attached, but little else. The salary he earns is just that, a "salary." He doesn't have to pay for his equipment or uniforms; those are supplied by his employer—the team. He doesn't have to pay for his shoes. As a matter of fact, a shoe company will probably pay him handsomely to wear their brand while he's working in the stadium where his games take place, the rent for which is paid by his employer—the team. He receives a sizable per diem for each day's food and incidentals, and his hotel and airfare are all paid for by his employer—the team. You see, the team is the producer of the product, the game, in which the ballplayer is playing. The athlete does not have to bear the expense of creating the product. After taxes he may have approximately $570,000 for personal use over the life of the "million-bucks" contract.

The exact opposite is true in the case of the music production company owner. You see, music production company owners are responsible for creating the product—the master recordings—and when they receive a million dollars from a major label, believe me, it ain't a million bucks. It's a million-dollar advance that is recoupable against future royalties they might earn, and has all kinds of strings attached—the strings of business overhead expenses. The music production company's million dollar contract may also be contingent upon the delivery of four LPs at $250,000 per LP, payable in installments of one-half ($125,000) upon commencement of recording of each LP and $125,000 upon satisfactory delivery of each LP. There are several more strings attached to the production company owner's "million dollars" as opposed to the athlete's "million bucks." The production company owner has to pay for office rent, telephone bills, lawyers, accountants, and more, in addition to paying the artist's, producer's, and songwriter's advances and royalties.

With all the expenses of running the production company business, the production company owner may end up with only $200,000 over the life of the "million-dollar" contract *before* personal income taxes. As you can see by the bottom-line comparison with the athlete, the difference is substantial. That's when you know, at least in the music business, "A Million Dollars Ain't a Million Bucks."

Having the proper perspective (while producing your powerful product) of the industry will help you to understand the necessity of conducting your business in conformance with the last Big P—**Professional Attitude.**

PROFESSIONAL ATTITUDE

The major record label has, as one of its many jobs, the responsibility of advancing hundreds of thousands of dollars to the music production company. As a result, it has to depend on the production company owner to handle his or her company's business in a fair and professional manner. The last thing a major label needs is for the production company to deliver master recordings only to find out, in the middle of the manufacturing process, that a producer, artist, or songwriter has a claim against the production company for failing to properly compensate them. This could occur if the production company fails to properly clear samples, pay recording costs, or obtain the complete rights to the masters. And believe me, even if you're acting as your own production company and label, recording and releasing your recordings on the Internet, you'd better heed this advice: it's imperative for you to be educated in the business and hire qualified, experienced professionals to help you carry on your business in a professional and businesslike fashion.

It's also the responsibility of the production company to have a business plan for success so that its employees and artists can feel confident they will be paid in a timely manner and to allow its managers to monitor their performance to ensure that they are working to achieve the company goals. All contracts should be drafted, negotiated, executed, and kept on file for future reference. There should be timely communication of vital information to the company's team members, which is important and crucial to projecting a positive image within the organization. With this type of internal display of "professional attitude," you'll garner respect which will ultimately have a positive effect on your success, both within your company and the other companies you do business with. These **Three Big P's** are the principles upon which successful production companies and musical careers should be established and maintained.

Remember, these are my keys to starting and growing a successful music venture.

> **POWERFUL PRODUCT,
> PROPER PERSPECTIVE,
> PROFESSIONAL ATTITUDE**

4

Choosing the Proper Business Structure for Your Production Company

Sole Proprietorship
General Partnership
Corporation
Limited Liability Company (LLC)

In order to start a successful music production company, it is first necessary to choose the proper business structure in which to operate. Keep in mind that the type of business structure that's good for you depends on a number of variables only you are aware of. The structure that's good for one company may not be good for another. After reading about the four recommended structures, make your choice based on *your* particular needs.

Sole proprietorships and general partnerships may be what you call "de facto" entities, which means that even though there may be no written organizational document identifying the business as such, the fact that the business exists and has the qualities of either a sole proprietorship or partnership may be enough for it to be legally recognized as one or the other under a state's law.

Sole Proprietorship. A sole proprietorship is an entity owned by an individual, called a sole proprietor. It may be a good way to do business—by yourself! No boss or partners to answer to. You make all the decisions and make all the profit. But, on the flip side, you bear the burden of all blame should things fail. Do you have to be a Mr. or Ms. Know-It-All to pursue success in this form of business? No! If you conduct your business in this manner, you can hire employees or consultants, accountants and lawyers to assist you in the business, provided these individuals have a clear understanding of their role, defined and documented through written agreements or letters of engagement identifying them as "hired help," not co-owners or partners. This is particularly important when dealing with close friends or relatives. It can be very easy for a brother, sister, cousin, or friend to "volunteer" services or money to establish your business. But, unless you have a written agreement clearly defining and limiting their role, they could, over time, consider themselves a co-owner of what you thought was your sole proprietorship. You might feel it's unnecessary to have written agreements with close friends and relatives, but keep in mind that if you don't, they could eventually sue you for an interest in what was once your business. While the sole proprietorship form of business may seem preferable, it also has its risks should the business experience financial difficulty.

A sole proprietor may be held personally liable for claims against his or her business. Suppose you, the sole proprietor, fail to, or are unable to, pay an outstanding business debt. Any of your personal assets held in your name may be seized and liquidated (sold to convert them to cash) to satisfy a judgment rendered against you as the result of a valid claim from a creditor.

As far as taxes are concerned, all profits and losses from your sole proprietorship must be accounted for on your personal tax return. So, if the expenses exceed the business's income for a particular tax year, your personal taxable income may be reduced accordingly. Of course, should your business show a profit, that profit may increase your taxable income. Thus, the sole proprietorship form of business may be particularly attractive to the new entrepreneur who anticipates investing significant amounts to get the business started and doesn't expect to receive profits from the business the first few years.

General Partnership. A general partnership is "an agreement between two or more individuals to conduct business for the purpose of making a profit." Does this agreement have to be in writing? No! A court can determine that a partnership exists based on either an express oral agreement of the partners or an implied agreement that is not spoken between the partners, but is manifested by the actions of the partners. For instance, Party A spends time finding talented songwriters, singers, and musicians and coordinating the production of demos to shop with a major label. Party B contributes monies to finance the operation and represents to others, with A's knowledge, that he or she is A's partner, an assertion which, at the time, A doesn't dispute. Should success occur and A attempts to deny the existence of a partnership, B may prevail in proving that an "implied" partnership existed, manifested by the parties' actions, and that he or she is entitled to a partnership share.

If you decide to do business with another party on a partnership basis, be sure to have the relationship well defined in the form of a proper written partnership agreement which should, among other things:

- ▶ Identify the proper names of the partners and the partnership;
- ▶ Define the roles of each partner—specifically, granting or limiting authority of each party to handle various phases of the business;
- ▶ Spell out the contribution each party is making to the partnership by way of money or services;

➤ Define the partners' interest in the partnership's profits and losses and partnership property;
➤ Denote the method of dissolving the partnership should a partner leave or die; this provision should spell out the method of valuation and payment of a leaving or deceased partner's share;
➤ Otherwise comply with partnership laws of the state in which you do business.

As with a sole proprietorship, individual partners are each subject to personal liability for partnership debts and, in most states, one partner may be forced to bear the entire debt of the partnership. In other words, a creditor of the partnership may choose to pursue the "deep pocket" partner (the one with the money) for all of the debt of the partnership. That's why it's important to have a written partnership agreement that should, among other things, give the "deep pocket" partner the right to proceed against the other partners for their share of debt should the "deep pocket" partner be "tapped" by a creditor.

A partner is treated just like a sole proprietor for tax purposes. A partner's share of any profit or loss of the partnership must be accounted for on her or his personal income tax returns. It is necessary for an informational partnership schedule to be attached to the partners' tax returns to justify the profit or loss. In this regard, the partnership should apply to the IRS for a TIN (tax identification number) to be used in referencing and filing the informational partnership schedule. A TIN may be obtained by filing a SS-4 form with the IRS, and it is usually necessary to start a bank account in the name of the partnership.

Is a partnership a good form of business for a music production company? Yes, if a properly prepared partnership contract is understood and executed by all partners, doing business as a partnership may be less costly than incorporating, where the ongoing, year-after-year costs of tax preparation, lawyer fees, and other expenses could run into thousands of dollars. The primary drawback of a partnership is that the partners may be subject to personal liability. However, in the case of a new production company, where the potential of liability is low and the probability that start-up expenses that can be written off against personal income is high, the partnership form of business may be the way to go.

Corporation. The corporation is the third form of business structure recommended for the production company. Whereas a sole proprietor or a general partner can be held personally liable for debts and claims against their business, a corporation is deemed, in the eyes of the law, as a third person or entity of its own which can be held liable for debts and claims independent from its owners, the shareholders. Therefore, if actions taken on behalf of a corporation lead to liability, only the corporation's assets, not the shareholders' personal assets, may be used to satisfy the liability. In other words, incorporating creates a corporate shield from liability, protecting the shareholders from being personally liable—*if* the corporation is properly doing business as a corporation.

Some people think that all you have to do to have a valid corporation is to file articles of incorporation with the state in which you're doing business. (That's as much a myth as the supposed rule that if you use no more than four (4) bars of another person's song, you can't be sued for copyright infringement.) If a corporation is sued and it becomes necessary to prove its validity, you will be expected to produce more than the registered articles of incorporation. In order to prove the existence of an ongoing corporation, a court could demand to see the corporate record book, which should contain by-laws, regulations, proof of notice of annual board and shareholder meetings, minutes of all those meetings, proper election of officers, proof of filing and paying state and federal corporation taxes, and so on. In other words, "articles of incorporation alone do not a corporation make!" If a corporation only files articles and otherwise has not conducted business as a valid corporation, the court may allow the corporate shield of liability to be pierced and the shareholders may be held personally liable for the corporation's debts or obligations. So, in order to get the full benefits of incorporation, you must also bear the expense of hiring attorneys and accountants to maintain the corporate books and records properly.

While incorporation may shield a shareholder from personal liability, it does result in double taxation. Any profit on the corporate level is taxed at corporate rates and then again on a personal level if and when any of corporate earnings are disbursed to shareholders as payment for services or as a dividend. However, if you meet certain qualifications and make the request within a specified time after incorporation, the IRS allows you to elect subchapter S status. This special tax designation status allows the corporation's shareholders to be treated like partners for tax purposes. The corporation pays no corporate tax on its profit. Instead, the corporation's profit is attributed to the shareholders' personal incomes, according to their ownership interests, and taxed accordingly. This election is recommended to newly-formed small corporations which expect losses in the first few years.

Most states allow corporations to elect to be "close corporations." Close corporations (see chart) usually have fewer than twenty to thirty shareholders and are allowed to conduct business on a less formal basis than a regular corporation. Close corporations restrict the unfettered trading of shares by requiring shareholders to first offer to sell their shares to other existing shareholders.

IRS SUBCHAPTER S STATUS

Purpose:	Allows corporations with few shareholders to whom most of the corporation income is distributed, the ability to be treated as if it were a partnership for income tax purposes, while retaining the corporate advantage of limited liability.
Qualifications:	In most states, less than thirty-five (35) shareholders who must, in most cases, be individuals (not other corporations or partnerships); S-corporation may have no more than one class of stock.

	CLOSE CORPORATION
Purpose:	Allows small corporation (where stock is held by a few individuals) the ability to manage its affairs on a less formal basis and restrict the transfer of shares to existing shareholders
Qualifications:	All shareholders must assent to terms of a close corporation agreement in writing. The close corporation agreement should, at least, contain provisions which: Provide for management of the close corporation. • possibly eliminating the board of directors entirely • delegating authority to directors, shareholders, officers, or other persons Specify voting requirements for action by the close corporation. • approval of corporate action by a certain number of shareholders Provide for corporate distribution of profit. • when dividends declared and/or profits shared Restrict issuance or transfer of shares. • limit transfer of shares to close corporation shareholders

The close corporation record book should contain a close corporation agreement, which should: (a) identify the officers; (b) delegate duties; and (c) outline the decision-making process, as well as the method of transferring shares between shareholders. Close corporation designation eases the burden of formalization and creates a mechanism allowing original shareholders to maintain control.

Limited Liability Company (LLC). The fourth form of recommended business entity, the limited liability company (LLC), has become a favorite among many entertainment business owners. In some circumstances, the limited liability company may combine the best features of a partnership and a corporation. The owners of an LLC are called "members," rather than shareholders (as in corporations) or partners (as in partnerships). One or more persons may form this type of entity, and by doing so, may limit their liability, as with a corporation, and receive the favorable tax aspects of doing business as a partnership. In most instances, an LLC member may not be held personally liable for obligations of the entity.

LLCs are treated the same as a partnership for tax purposes. All profit and losses of the LLC are apportioned and passed through to the members' personal incomes for taxing or deduction purposes.

In order to form an LLC, most states require the filing of a simple document, referred to as articles of organization. In all instances, in addition to the articles of organization, it is advisable to have an "operating agreement" between the members that, much like a partnership agreement, sets forth the rights, duties, and responsibilities of the LLCs members and/or managers.

5

The Across the Board Deal

How to Maximize Income for Your Production Company

I'm sure when most of you looked at this book's table of contents, you wondered what an "across the board deal" was. It is the contractual method, sometimes referred to as the blessed trinity of contracts, where a manager or production company signs an artist for management, production, and publishing. It became a popular way to sign artists in the 1970s when managers, who spent a great deal of money to finance the recording, wardrobe, grooming, and sometimes living expenses of artists, sought a way to participate in as many incoming producing activities of artists as possible in order to recoup their investment as quickly as possible. Today, most artists' lawyers would advise their clients not to enter into such agreements because of the inherent potential of conflict of interest caused by managers putting their interest before those of the artist. This can result in the manager "double dipping" or profiting twice—from producing the artist's recordings, and publishing the artist's compositions and commissioning the advances and royalties due the artist from these activities. Artist managers initiated the practice of signing artists to across the board deals years ago, and since then many production companies have adopted it; they sign artists to record demos in order to seek label deals and their principals establish related management companies or divisions to handle the affairs of their artists. While most artists' attorneys may not recommend that their clients enter into this type of arrangement, some production company lawyers still see it as the best way to maximize the revenue potential of an artist to the production company. While I can understand the artist's attorney not wanting a client to enter into this type of arrangement, in certain cases, where the production company is properly run by individuals with the expertise to properly market and promote the acts' recordings, publishing interests, and live performances to a particular genre, an artist may be best served by entering such agreements.

In my experience, most new artists signed to production companies rely on the companies to not only record them, but also to handle various aspects of their business that they may be unfamiliar with. So, if a production company signs a new artist to a recording agreement, it is probable that the artist will also need the company's help and assistance in other areas, such as developing a stage show or arranging the engagement of a booking agent to secure performance dates. If the artist is also a songwriter or has the potential to become a songwriter, he or she may also rely on the production company to do such things as registering their copyrights with the Copyright Office, place songs with other artists, and collect any royalties due the artist from the exploitation of his or her compositions.

If your production company has this type of relationship with one of its artists, you may already have an undocumented "across the board" relationship. The next step is to convert this relationship into an agreement, reduced to writing in order to clarify the specific terms of the relationship.

This method of signing and working with (and on behalf of) the artist in multiple capacities may also result in the production company maximizing the return on its investment in the artist's career. If the production company sells the artist's records independently or through a major label, the value of the artist's copyrights will be enhanced. The exposure the artist receives from radio play and streaming of their records may also result in the artist receiving more requests for paid live performance dates. In other words, the artist may receive multiple benefits from the production company choosing to record the artist. So, why shouldn't the production company be able to share in the other sources of revenue, such as publishing royalties and live performance fees generated by the artist? Well, with an across the board deal, the production company can, if certain guidelines are adhered to.

First, the production company must decide whether the increased responsibility which comes along with a commitment to provide these additional services to the artist is worth the time and headache. As we will discuss in the review of the management agreement, the management business can be a very lonely, time-consuming, and aggravating business with little reward, unless and until the artist has achieved a significant amount of success.

Administering the copyrights of the artist is also very complicated and tedious work that can cause a production company owner to wonder: Is it worth the time and headache? Yes, because, as you'll read in my chapter on copyright principles, the copyright is the most valuable asset in the music business. The production company owner must realize that the music industry is a hit or miss business. I once heard someone say, "You can't make a living in the music business, you can only make a killing! The object is to put as many killings together as you can." I disagree with this saying. There are undoubtedly a number of ways to make a decent living in the music business. However, investing time and money in this business certainly involves a significant amount of risk. The chances of failure are great, but, if your artists become the next viral sensation, hit the top of the charts, selling-out records, performances, and merchandise, you certainly want to be in a position to participate in as many streams of revenue as possible.

In an across the board deal, the production company concurrently signs the artist to an exclusive recording artist agreement, a co-publishing and administration agreement, an exclusive songwriter agreement, and a management agreement. (The agreements will be discussed and analyzed through the remainder of this book.)

As noted in the following diagram, I recommend using different names for the production company's publishing and management operations for purposes of clarifying each operation's function, as well as creating separate accounting systems for each.

Also, in order to make this type of relationship stand up under a challenge in court, it is important to adhere to a few rules to counter an artist's challenge that the production company's involvement on so many levels is overreaching, and otherwise too burdensome to the artist and may, therefore, be deemed a breach of the fiduciary duty the production company's management company owes to the artist.

First, make sure that the agreements run concurrently and are coterminous, so that when one contract ends, they all end. Second, the management agreement should specify that no management commission be taken on earnings due the artist from the production company or publishing company. Third, the production company should co-publish, on a 50-50 basis, the artist's

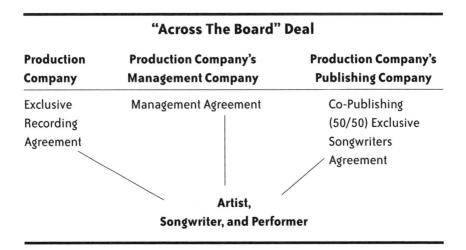

copyrights under the terms of a co-publishing and administration contract. If the production company attempts to take 100% of the artist's copyright interests or takes a management commission on the artist's earnings made pursuant to an agreement with the production company or its other affiliates, the validity of the across the board deal may be jeopardized. In other words, the production company's management division may not take a commission on the artist's advances or royalties that are due the artist from the management company's production affiliate. The same is true of advances and royalties due the artist from the production company's publishing affiliate.

In conclusion, although the across the board deal may present a challenge to the production company, it is its best hope of maximizing its return on investing in the development of an artist's career. The artist, on the other hand, must carefully evaluate the personnel and structure of a production company that presents it with a set of "across the board" agreements. If the artist recognizes a "weak link" in the production, publishing, or management "chain" of the company proposing the deal, he or she should attempt to negotiate separate agreements upon more favorable terms with only the divisions of the company that are determined to be capable to do a credible job of advancing their career.

6

The New Business Model

A Look at the 360° Deal—Labels and More Venture "Across the Board"

Shortly after the turn of the century, I was negotiating a matter with a record production/publishing company regarding my client's copyright interests in songs. I was seeking to obtain a percentage ownership interest on behalf of my clients in some compositions written and produced by the record company's principals. At some point during the negotiations, the company lawyer said, "You know John, my clients only write the songs and produce the recordings. That's the only income they participate in and, as a result of their writing and producing hit songs, your clients have had a long and prosperous career selling out live performances, attracting endorsements, sponsorships, acting in movies and other activities that generate revenue my clients don't have the right to participation in. Maybe my clients should participate in these other forms of your client's revenue since you now want your clients to participate in theirs. After all, it was my client's hit songs and production talents that made them stars." That was the first time I heard a record label representative talk about sharing in an artist's revenue beyond what was generated from recording and publishing.

Early this century, major labels made a necessary change in their business model. Not only did they have to adapt to their recordings being consumed in the digital format, they also had to change their contractual relationships with artists to remain in business. As a result of the impact of MP-3s, Napster and P2P file-sharing, record companies took drastic steps to decrease their expenses and increase their shrinking revenue base. Massive employee layoffs and trimming of their artist rosters soon followed and after the rapid and steep decline in the sale of albums after the year 2000, labels recognized the necessity of participating in artist earnings beyond just selling or licensing recordings. In 2002 EMI signed European superstar, Robbie Williams, to the first major label "all-rights" agreement or 360° deal, which allowed the label to participate in the full circle—360 degrees—of William's earnings in the entertainment industry, including live performance, publishing, merchandising, sponsorships, acting gigs, etc., and not just in revenue generated from the sale and use of his recordings. Shortly thereafter most major labels and even some live promotion companies followed suit. By the end of the new millennium's first decade the world's largest live promotion company, Live Nation, entered the fray, signing 360° deals with Madonna, Jay-Z, Shakira, Nickelback and others.

More and more artists are experiencing success beyond their recording and live performing endeavors. Beyonce is not only a hit-making recording artist and songwriter, she's also a movie actress, endorsement specialist for such varied products as Pepsi, House of Dereon fashions, L'Oreal and others. As a member of Destiny's Child, she signed with Columbia Records in the mid 1990s, at a time when such labels were not insisting on 360° deals. While the Columbia executives at that time could not have predicted Napster or the P2P file-sharing debacle would surface at the turn of the century, you can bet in hindsight, they would have profited immensely from an "all rights" deal with each individual member of the group (which also included pop star Kelly Rowland and gospel performer, Michelle Williams.)

The concept of an all-rights agreement between a label and recording artist is not new. In fact, in the sixties several labels employed this strategy. In the 1960s the in-house Motown artist management company, International Talent Management, Inc. headed by Shelly Berger, managed all the Motown artists. In addition, Motown's publishing affiliate, Jobete, published the compositions written by their artist-songwriters and produced their TV Specials and movies like "Lady Sings the Blues" and "Mahogany." I'm sure that if endorsements and sponsorships were prevalent at that time, Motown would have arranged and participated in a deal to have a "David Ruffin" line of fashion glasses with an eyeglass manufacturer long before there were the celebrity lines we see on store shelves today. David, the lead singer of the chart-topping group The Temptations, would wear several different eyeglass styles and was quite the fashion trendsetter in that regard in the sixties.

Although during the latter part of the last century major labels refrained from forcing their artist-songwriters to sign co-publishing agreements with the label's affiliated publishing companies, many independent production companies entered into "across the board deals" with the artists they signed. From the 70s through the current day, several production companies and managers enter into the "the blessed trinity" of contracts that give them the rights not only to artist's recordings, but also co-publishing interests in their compositions and management commissions on the artist's other revenue streams. Label 360° agreements now mirror these deals and, unless a new artist has several labels vying for its services, it's unlikely that such an artist will receive the million dollar advances superstar artists like Jay-Z and others earn. In fact, as a part of their 360° deals, along with a hefty advance, many superstar artists may even receive an ownership interest in the master recordings. However, an unproven new artist may be offered a development or singles' deal that limits the label's risk by committing the

> In fact, as part of their 360° deals, along with a hefty advance, many superstar artists may even receive an ownership interest in the master recordings.

payment of only a small artist advance and recording costs for only three-four demos or singles. If the label determines that the artist's demos are satisfactory or the public reacts favorably to a single release, they would then have the option to enter into a multiple album 360-degree deal with the artist upon terms outlined in the development or singles agreement.

Just like in the case of across the board deals, many artists vehemently oppose these types of agreements but, in most cases, acquiesce to the label's demands to pay an artist's royalty of 13%–16% of the wholesale price, sometimes referred to as, Published Price per Dealer (PPD), and a 10%-25% share of the artist's other ancillary revenues dependent on whether the label undertakes a passive or active role in these income generating activities. For instance, while a label may not insist that the artist sign a co-publishing agreement with its publishing affiliate wherein the affiliate administers the artists compositions and receives up to 25%–30% of earnings from exploitation of the copyrights, it may request the first right and matching rights to negotiate such a deal with the artist. In that case, the artist is required to try to reach a deal with the label's publishing affiliate before seeking an agreement with a third party publisher. If the label and artist can't come to an agreement, the artist may then pursue an offer from a third party, but if successful with that effort, the artist must give the label's publishing affiliate the right to match the competing offer before executing the third party deal. Label first and matching right provisions may also apply to other ancillary income revenue activities, like merchandising, video and film opportunities, etc. Artist representatives try to limit the label's take on each revenue source, particularly in the case where the label offers little or no assistance in generating income from these activities. This passive involvement is what is so objectionable to artists. After all, why should the company participate in earnings they did nothing to help create? As a result of these complaints, labels have begun to develop special departments and/or merge with companies that specialize in ancillary income activities. For instance, Universal

Music both partnered with a Live Nation artist management company, Frontline Management, and merged with Bravo Merchandising in an effort to become more actively engaged in these two important income-generating areas of the business.

360° deals are becoming a staple in the business. But that does not mean that every new artist has to sign one. If an artist has several labels competing to sign them, they may use that leverage to sign with a label on more traditional terms. It may not happen often, but it is possible.

7

Contracts and Accounting Statements

Introduction

Now it's time to begin the review of the contracts, samples of which follow.

A contract is a binding agreement between two or more parties and, depending upon a number of factors such as the subject matter of the contract, may be verbal or written. In the music business, it is advisable for all your agreements to be in writing. I must emphasize that the sample contracts and accountings that follow are exactly that—samples. In fact, I disagree with many provisions in some of them, but included them here to point out these deficiencies. In other words, don't consider these "standard contracts." During my years of practice, I have drafted, altered, and negotiated hundreds of contracts. What never ceases to amaze me is how they are all different in some form or fashion. One of the first things professors in law school tell you is how dynamic and ever-changing the field of law is. And were they right? You bet! There may be a few "boiler plate" provisions in every contract, but minor alterations could change the meaning entirely. There is no such thing as standard in today's business. The business is changing so rapidly that, a contract that may have been adequate six months ago may be outdated today. Therefore, while these samples serve as a basis for discussion, they are not, by any means, recommended for a company's or client's specific use, without proper review and revision by an experienced, qualified professional.

Exclusive recording (360° deal), songwriter, co-publishing and *administration*, and *management* contracts follow. The actual contract is on the left side of the page with my comments on the right side of the page. Make sure you read the *entire* contract to get a feel for the language of industry terms and contractual provisions. The comments I've made break down the legalese for you and offer some key hints to understanding and improving some of the provisions.

The statement of recording, copyright, and management earnings is designed to help you see how the money, committed to in the contracts, flows through these contracts to the accounting statements. The contractual provisions related to the accounting entries may be indicated for your reference. The analysis following the statement is designed to help you see how the contract serves as the faucet, wherein each contract provision acts as a handle, turning on, or in many cases, closing the valves, through which the money flows to the production company, artist, and songwriter.

8

Exclusive Recording Artist Contract

Analysis of Artist/Production Company 360° Agreement

CONTRACT

Exclusive Recording Artist Agreement with Production Company

AGREEMENT made as of the __ day of _____, by and between _____ (herein called "Company"), c/o _____ and _____ herein called "Artist"), c/o _____

WITNESSETH:

1. <u>TERM</u>

   (a) The term hereof (the "Term") shall consist of an initial

ANALYSIS

Analysis of Exclusive Recording Agreement

1. The term or length of time the agreement may be enforced has been the subject of significant controversy over the past twenty (20) years. In the

CONTRACT

period (the "First Contract Period") plus the additional "Contract Periods," if any, by which such Term may be extended by Company's exercise of one or more of the options granted to Company below (unless otherwise extended or suspended as provided herein).

(b) You hereby irrevocably grant to Company three (3) separate consecutive options to extend the Term for a Second, Third and Fourth Contract Period, respectively. The above-stated option periods will be deemed adjusted in accordance with any applicable recording agreement pertaining to the distribution and marketing of records made hereunder between a third-party record label or distributor ("Distributor") and Company. Each such option shall be deemed to be exercised by Company unless it shall give you written notice to the contrary prior to the date that the then-current Contract Period would otherwise expire.

(c) The First Contract Period shall commence on the date hereof and shall continue until the earlier of: (I) the date nine (9) months after the delivery to Company of the Minimum Recording Commitment for such Contract Period, or (ii) if applicable, thirty (30) days after the date on which the Distributor exercises its option for the Second Contract Period a copy of which shall be provided to you. Each subsequent Contract Period shall commence on

ANALYSIS

early 1980's, a standard recording agreement may have had a term of one (1) year, with four (4) one-year options. However, during each contract year the artist was expected to deliver, at a minimum, one (1) album with the record company having the option to request an additional (option) album per contract year. Upon the record company exercising its option to the additional album, the term of the contract year would be extended a certain period of time (usually six–nine months) following the delivery of the option album. This caused some artists to think they had a five-year contract when, in actuality, as a result of other fine print provisions in the contract, the record company was allowed to extend the contract up to ten (10) years or longer. The artist Prince entered into one of these agreements with Warner Bros. Records in 1977 and was bound to the agreement well into the 1990's when he finally worked out a release from the agreement wherein, it was reported, Warner Brothers waived its rights to the final two (2) albums due under the original and/or renegotiated contract. Prince became vocal about his plight and was one of the original organizers of the Artist Empowerment Coalition (a group of artists and other interested parties) that lobbied the state legislature in California and New York to consider legislation limiting the length of exclusive recording agreements to seven years. While these legislative measures were never enacted into law, the public outcry and support of other groups, like the Recording Artist

CONTRACT

the date following the date of expiration of the immediately preceding Contract Period and shall continue until the earlier of: (i) the date nine (9) months after the Delivery to Company of the Minimum Recording Commitment for such Contract Period, or (ii) if applicable, thirty (30) days after the date on which the Distributor exercises its option for the next Contract Period.

(i) Notwithstanding anything to the contrary contained herein, you shall have the right to terminate the Term of this Agreement by giving written notice thereof to Company at any time after a date twenty-four (24) months from the date hereof unless, prior to the date of such notice, Company has entered into or substantially negotiated the major provisions of an agreement with a record company (referred to herein as the "Distributor"): (A) which is a parent or subsidiary of, or is affiliated with one of the major "branch" distributors in the United States (i.e., SONY, UMG, WMG, etc.) or (B) A major independent record company (i.e., E1, etc.) or (C) whose records are distributed by any such record company, pursuant to which such Distributor shall have the right to distribute in the United States and Canada records embodying Master Recording produced hereunder (said agreement is herein referred to as the "Distribution Agreement"). Upon such termination, all parties shall be deemed to have

ANALYSIS

Coalition (RAC) was enough to convince major labels to shorten the length of time of these agreements so that the normal term is four (4) to six (6) contract periods in which the minimum delivery requirement during each period is one (1) album. Each contract period usually lasts the longer of 12 months from the commencement of the period or nine (9) to twelve (12) months following the date of delivery of the album due during the period. This contract's term is one initial period, plus three (3) option periods and states that each option period ends nine (9) months following the delivery of the album due each period. However, if an artist has leverage (i.e., a past record of significant sales), the end date of each period may be negotiated to five (5) to seven (7) months following delivery. Paragraph 1 (c) indicates that, if the Production Company enters an agreement with a record distribution company and the terms of that agreement are longer than this one (i.e., five (5) or six (6) periods), the term of this agreement will be extended until the time of the termination of the distribution agreement. Paragraph 1 (c)(i) gives the artist the very important right to terminate the agreement if the Production company has failed to enter or substantially negotiate an agreement with a major big three (SONY, WMG or UMG) or major independent record distributor within twenty-four (24) months from date of this agreement. This gives the artist a way to get out the agreement if the Production Company isn't able to get obtain a

CONTRACT

fulfilled all of their obligations hereunder; and

(ii) Notwithstanding any language to the contrary contained herein, should the first or any subsequent Distribution Agreement, as defined above, terminate prior to the date on which this Agreement would expire if all options hereunder were exercised, then the current Contract Period and the Term of this Agreement shall automatically be deemed suspended until the date on which the Company enters into or substantially negotiates a new Distribution Agreement with a new Distributor. Notwithstanding the foregoing, any such suspension shall not continue for more than eighteen (18) months provided that you cooperate with Company, at Company's reasonable request and expense, for the recording of a minimum of five (5) demonstration tapes or Master Recordings for use in securing a new Distribution Agreement. In the event that no Distribution Agreement has been concluded or substantially negotiated within the said eighteen (18) month suspension, this Agreement shall be terminated and all parties shall be deemed to have fulfilled all of their obligations hereunder.

(d) In the event you terminate the Term as set forth in this paragraph l(c)(i) or (ii) above and you secure a recording agreement within eighteen (18) months following the date of such termination,

ANALYSIS

significant outlet for distribution of the artist's records. If the agreement between the Production Company and the distributor should end prematurely, Paragraph 1 (c)(ii) states that the contract will be suspended for up to eighteen (18) months to extend the Production company time to obtain an agreement with another record distributor. However, Paragraph 1. (d) gives the artist the right to seek their own agreement with another company provided the artist reimburses the Production Company for costs of any demos they paid for and used to secure a deal with another company.

CONTRACT	ANALYSIS
then you shall reimburse Company for all documented costs and expenses incurred in connections with the Demos created by Company in its efforts to secure the Distribution Agreement (the "Demo Costs") and any documented out-of-pocket promotion, marketing, audition and other miscellaneous costs incurred by Company out of the first monies paid to you pursuant to any such Distribution agreement.	
2. RECORDING SERVICES (a) During the Term of this Agreement, you shall render to Company your exclusive services as a recording artist for the purpose of making Master Recordings and as otherwise set forth herein. (b) Artist shall be free to render services in the recording industry as a "side person" as that term is commonly understood in the recording industry (subject to the provision of a standard courtesy credit on behalf of Company) and pursuant to paragraph 10(b)(i) herein.	2. (a) During the term of this agreement, the artist provides its exclusive services for the recording and production of records to the Production Company. This means that the Artist will record for no one other than the Company during the term of agreement. If the Artist performs as a guest artist on another label, he/she cannot do so without the permission of the Production Company. Being a guest artist on another artist's recording is very common now and the provisions of Paragraph 2. (b) of this contract allow the artist to provide services as a "side person" (i.e. provide background vocal or instrumental performances) on another company's recordings provided the Production Company receives standard courtesy credit on behalf of the company.
3. RECORDING COMMITMENT (a) During each Contract Period, you shall render your services to Company, in accordance with the terms and conditions hereof, in connection with	3. During the initial period, the artist's minimum recording commitment is one (1) master recording. However the Production Company has the right and option to require the artist to record either a second master recording or an album during this period.

CONTRACT

recording the minimum numbers of Masters (the "Minimum Recording Commitment") set forth in the following schedule:

CONTRACT PERIOD	MINIMUM RECORDING COMMITMENT
First	One (1) Master/ One (I) Album
Second	One (1) Album
Third	One (I) Album
Fourth	One (1) Album

(b) During the First Contract Period, Company shall have the exclusive and irrevocable right and option to require you to render your services in connection with the recording of one (1) additional Master (the "Second Single"). Company may request the Second Single at any time prior to the date on which the First Contract Period would otherwise expire. During the First Contract Period, Company shall also have the exclusive and irrevocable right and option to require you to render your services in connection with recording such additional Masters as may be desirable to constitute an Album (the "First Album"). Company may request the First Album at any time prior to the date on which the First Contract Period would otherwise expire, and it is understood that Company may request the First Album in addition to or in lieu of the Second Single. If Company so requests the Second Single and/or the

ANALYSIS

During each of the three (3) option-periods, the Artist must deliver one (1) album. Should the Production Company exercise an option, the Artist shall record and deliver the album within one-hundred twenty (120) days following the commencement of each contract period. Artist is also required to perform for the making of audio-visuals recordings (videos).

CONTRACT

First Album, such Second Single and/or the First Album shall be deemed to be part of the Minimum Recording Commitment for the First Contract Period.

(c) You agree that you shall complete your Minimum Recording Commitment for each Contract Period within one hundred and twenty (120) days following the commencement of such Contract Period.

(d) Subject to your prior professional commitments, you shall perform for Company for the purposes of making audiovisual recordings and shall, without limitation of your obligations as *set* forth elsewhere in this Agreement, comply with all terms and conditions relating thereto as may be set forth in any Distribution Agreement, provided you are given the relevant portions of the Distribution Agreement to which you are to be bound.

4. RECORDING PROCEDURE

(a) In connection with Master Recordings to be made hereunder, the following matters shall be mutually determined by Company and Artist:

(i) Selection of producer;

(ii) Selection of material to be recorded (including the number of compositions to be recorded); and

ANALYSIS

4. Prior to the commencement of each recording session, the Production Company and Artist must mutually approve such things as, the selection of a producer and financial terms of employment of producer and the selection of the material and dates and location of the recording. If the Production Company and Artist have a dispute about these matters, the Production Company shall have final say and Paragraph 4.(b) provides that each master recording is subject to the Production Company's approval as both,

CONTRACT

(iii) Selection of dates of rehearsal/recording and studio where recording is to take place, including the cost of recording therein. The scheduling and booking of all studio time will be done by Company in consultation with Artist.

(iv) Notwithstanding the foregoing, in the event of a dispute, however, Company shall maintain final decision-making rights.

(b) Each Master Recording made hereunder shall be subject to Company's approval as technically and commercially satisfactory for the manufacture and sale of Phonograph Records.

(c) (i) Each Album constituting your Minimum Recording Commitment shall consist of at least ten (10) Masters with a duration of at least thirty-five (35) minutes, unless Company agrees otherwise.

(ii) No "live" recording will apply in fulfillment of your Minimum Recording Commitment unless approved in writing by Company, nor will Company be required to make any payment in connection with any such recordings except any royalties which may become due if same released by Company.

5. RECORDING COSTS

(a) Company (or Distributor) will pay all specifically approved Recording Costs in connection with

ANALYSIS

technically and commercially satisfactory. These measures may seem extreme, but in most cases, particularly for new recording artists, the Company may be in the best position to determine what's best in this regard. However, artists with a proven track record of success may be able to negotiate out the "commercially satisfactory" requirement.

5. The Production Company will pay all prior-approved recording costs. However, under this paragraph, the Artist is responsible for any costs that exceed the budget amounts that are

CONTRACT	ANALYSIS
Master Recordings made hereunder. Notwithstanding the foregoing, you shall be solely responsible for paying any Recording Costs incurred by Company or the Distributor which are in excess of the recording budget approved by Company and Distributor and which are solely caused by your failure to appear or perform at scheduled recording sessions or your failure to otherwise perform your obligations hereunder. You shall reimburse Company for any such costs or, at Company's discretion, Company may deduct an amount equal to such excess costs from your royalties, and advances hereunder. You shall not incur any Recording Costs without Company's prior approval. (b) Nothing contained in this Agreement shall obligate Company to permit the continuation of any recording session to be held in connection with Master Recordings hereunder, if Company reasonably anticipates that the Master Recordings being recorded will not be satisfactory.	caused by the Artist's failure to appear or perform at the sessions. Therefore, it is mandatory for the Artist to be mindful of the third Big P, Professional Attitude, when recording because any act like being late for sessions or causing sessions to extend beyond their scheduled times may cause the payment of excess costs which the Artist must bear. In addition, if the Production Company reasonably anticipates that recording will not be satisfactory, it may pull the plug, so to speak . . . cut off the funding of the sessions.
6. ADVANCES (a) All monies paid to you, or on your behalf, pursuant to or in connection with the Agreement (other than royalties paid pursuant to Paragraphs 8, 13, 18 or 20 hereof), including Recording Costs, shall constitute Advances unless otherwise expressly agreed in writing by an authorized officer of Company.	6. All monies paid to, or on behalf of the Artist in connection with the agreement, including recording costs, are considered advances and therefore recoupable (deducted from) any monies, including royalties, that are due the Artist. Other costs including, but not limited to video costs, independent promotion costs, tour support are also considered advances and recouped from the Artist's record royalty

CONTRACT

(b) Conditioned upon your full and faithful performance of all of the terms and conditions hereof and upon Company's receipt from Distributor, Company shall pay to you the following minimum Advances (which shall be inclusive of any "scale" payments due you under any applicable union or guild agreements) in respect of each Album required to be recorded by you hereunder, in each case, promptly following the delivery of such Album to Company.

CONTRACT PERIOD	ADVANCE
First- First Single-	$ 10,000.00
Second Single-	$ 10,000.00
Album-	$ 30,000.00
Second Album-	$ 75,000.00
Third Album-	$125,000.00
Fourth Album-	$150,000.00

(c) The Advance payable in connection with the First Contract Period hereunder shall be paid as follows:

(i) Fifty (50%) percent promptly after Company enters into the first Distribution Agreement and is paid the Advance from the Distributor and the full execution of this Agreement and the balance promptly following the delivery to and acceptance by Company (or Distributor) of such Master Album.

(ii) The Advance payable with respect to subsequent

ANALYSIS

account. However, if an artist has any kind of leverage, they should be able to negotiate recoupment of only 50% of video and independent promotion costs. Paragraph 6. (b) deals with the Artist advance and is one of the most serious concerns for the Artist. I recommend you always, always ask for an advance beyond the amount of the recording costs, so you have money to live on during the recording process and period of time it takes for your record to be released and (hopefully) become successful. I wish I could say the amounts of the advances offered in this contract are low. But, unfortunately, due to continued decreasing album sales, these amounts are reasonable for even a major label artist with no leverage. However, having an established audience or a significant social media presence may increase your chances of negotiating higher advance amounts for both singles and albums. While this contract specifies that advances shall be paid one-half (1/2) upon commencement of recording and the balance upon delivery of the recording, some companies may be willing to pro-rate the advance and pay it on a monthly installment basis over a year or so that the artist may pay its monthly bills during the recording process.

CONTRACT

Contract Periods shall be payable with one-half (1/2) promptly following the commencement of recording of the Album comprising the Minimum Recording Commitment for such Contract Period, and the balance promptly following the delivery to and acceptance by Company (or Distributor) of such Album.

(d) Each of the Advances paid to you pursuant to this Paragraph 6, as well as all Recording Costs, shall be fully recoupable from any and all royalties (excluding mechanicals) payable under this Agreement.

(e) Any penalties charged to Company due to the late delivery to the Distributor of Masters hereunder, which late delivery was caused by reasons solely within your control, (other than such penalties due solely to Company's fault) shall be your responsibility, and Company shall have the right to deduct the amount of such penalties from any sums due hereunder.

7. GRANT OF RIGHTS

(a) All Master Recordings recorded hereunder and all Master Recordings embodying your performances which are recorded during the Term hereof, from the inception of recording thereof, and ail Phonograph Records manufactured therefrom, together with the performances embodied thereon (but not the musical compositions

ANALYSIS

7. In this paragraph, the Production Company claims that the Artist's performances on the recordings are "works for hire" or if not, the Artist assigns his/her rights in the copyright to the Production Company. A discussion of the significance of a work being designated a "work for hire" is thoroughly discussed in paragraph 6. of the songwriter's agreement. Equally important is the Artist's grant of rights to manufacture the recordings and

CONTRACT	ANALYSIS
embodied thereon), shall be the sole property of Company and its designees (including, without limitation, Distributor) throughout the world, free from any claims whatsoever by you or any other Person; and Company (and its designees) shall have the exclusive right to copyright such Master Recordings (excluding the underlying musical compositions embodied thereon) in its name as the owner and author thereof and to secure any and all renewals and extensions of such copyright. Solely for the purposes of any applicable copyright law, all such Master Recordings (excluding the underlying musical compositions embodied thereon) shall be deemed "work made for hire" and owned by Company (and its designees). If for any reason, such Master Recordings are determined not to be "works for hire", then all rights, titles and interest therein and thereto including all copyrights therein, but explicitly excluding the rights, titles and interest in and to the underlying musical compositions embodied thereon, are hereby deemed irrevocably transferred to Company (and its designees). (b) Without limiting the generality of the foregoing, Company and any Person authorized by Company (including Distributor) shall have the unlimited right, throughout the world, to manufacture Phonograph Records and other derivatives by any method now or hereafter known, delivered from the Master	other derivatives by any method now or hereafter known to the Production Company. This provision is inserted to protect the Production Company and/or Distribution Company from claims filed by several artists from the 1960 – 70's in lawsuits brought early this century alleging that the standard recording agreements they signed during the 1960's and 1970's did not contemplate the sale of recordings on anything other than physical objects, like vinyl, cassettes, or CD's (e.g., not the Internet). A production company for Eminem even filed a similar case against Universal Music Group disputing the way Universal computed royalties for sale of digital downloads. The case primarily concerned whether a recording sold in digital format should be considered a license or a sale. Most artists' contracts indicate that the artist gets a royalty of fifty percent (50%) for a license but only thirteen to sixteen percent (13–16%) for a sale. The case was eventually settled but not before a lower court decided that digital music should be treated as a license rather than a sale for royalty purposes. However, younger artists are not likely to be affected by the decision because since the early 2000s most record companies have revised of their contracts to include digital downloads among an artist's regular record sales and thereby subject to payment of the lower royalty rates. The Production Company also requires the artist to allow it to use the Artist's professional name, biographical information and likeness in the promotion of recordings.

CONTRACT

Recordings made hereunder, and to sell, market, transfer or otherwise deal in the same under any trademarks, names and labels, or to refrain from such manufacture, sale and dealing.

(c) Company and any Person authorized by Company (including Distributor) each shall have the right, and may grant to others the rights, to reproduce, print, publish or disseminate in any medium your approved name, approved portraits, approved pictures, approved likenesses and approved biographical material concerning you, as news or information, or for the purposes of trade, or for advertising purposes in connection with the exploitation of Masters recorded hereunder; provided, however, that no direct endorsement by you of any product or service shall be used without your prior written consent, said written consent not to be unreasonably withheld. During the Term of this Agreement, you shall not authorize any Party other than Company to use your name or likeness in connection with the advertising or sale of Phonograph Records (subject to paragraph 2(b) above). As used in this Agreement, "name" shall include any professional names or sobriquets. Any such approvals shall be exercised to the extent and in accordance with such procedures in respect thereof as may be set forth in the Distribution Agreement provided however that Artists is given the relevant portions of such

ANALYSIS

CONTRACT

Distribution Agreement relating to same.

8. ROYALTIES

Conditioned upon your full and faithful performance of all the terms and conditions hereof, you shall be paid royalties on net sales of Records derived from the Masters recorded hereunder, and other exploitations of the Masters, as hereinafter set forth:

(a) (i) On net sales of Albums sold at full price through normal retail channels in the United States ("USNRC Net Sales") the royalty rate shall be the following applicable percentage of the retail list price:

(A) On Albums derived from Masters recorded during the First and Second Contract Periods: Twelve (12%) percent.

(B) On Albums derived from Masters recorded during the Third and Fourth Contract Periods: Thirteen (13%) percent.

(ii) If USNRC Net Sales, on which royalties are payable pursuant to paragraph 8(a)(i) above, of any Album recorded in fulfillment of your Minimum Recording Commitment hereunder shall exceed 500,000 units, then the royalty rate shall be increased by the greater of one-half (1/2) of Company's royalty increase pursuant to the

ANALYSIS

8. Equally important to the issue of advances is the Artist's royalty rate. This paragraph provides for the Artist to receive a basic Album royalty rate of twelve percent (12%) of the retail list price during the first two contract periods and thirteen (13%) for the last two periods with escalations of the greater of one-half percent (½%) the Production Company's royalty increase pursuant to its Distribution Agreement or one-quarter percent (¼%) for sales in excess of 500,000 units for that particular album. In addition, there shall be a similar escalation for sales in excess of 1,000,000 units. In respect to Singles (physical or digital), the royalty rate shall be 12%. This rate is a little low. Most new artist royalty rates range between 13%–16% and, at least at major labels, are paid on the wholesale price (price per dealer (commonly referred to as PPD). For records that are not sold through normal retail channels, CDs and other sales for which the Production Company is paid a reduced royalty, the Artist's royalties are reduced in the same proportion as the Company's royalties are reduced. Most major labels only pay 75% of the basic royalty rates for the sale of CDs and other "new media" configurations of recordings. That's right, the royalty rate for albums in CD and digital download configurations will not be 12% as stated in paragraph 2, but 9% instead. A little unfair, huh? Well, unfortunately, some record companies take the hard line in

CONTRACT

Distribution Agreement or one-quarter of one percent (1/4%), for such sales of that particular Album in excess of 500,000 units. The royalty rate shall be increased by the greater of one-half (1/2) of Company's royalty increase pursuant to the Distribution Agreement or an additional one-quarter of one percent (1/4%) for such sales of that particular Album in excess of 1,000,000 units.

(iii) On USNRC Net Sales of Seven 7-inch, Twelve 12-inch Singles and as digital downloads, the royalty rate shall be Twelve (12%) percent.

(b) With respect to sales of Records other than USNRC Net Sales of Albums and Singles (including without limitation, sales outside the United States, club sales, mid-price and budget records, EP's, audiovisual records, etc.), and with respect to compact discs and other Records sold through normal retail channels as to which Company is paid a reduced royalty or is subject to a reduced basis your royalty shall be reduced in the same proportion as Company's royalty therefor is reduced pursuant to the Distribution Agreement. For the avoidance of doubt, if Company's royalty is not reduced by the Distributor, your royalty shall not be reduced under this Agreement.

(c) With respect to sales of Records or other uses of the Masters

ANALYSIS

negotiating this point. These types of provisions were first inserted into agreements in the 1980's when record companies argued that they should pay a reduced royalty on the (then new configuration) CD to compensate for the investment the companies made in developing the CD and building plants to manufacture them. However, over the past 30 years the companies have more than recouped their investment and as a result, most artist attorneys maintain this argument no longer "holds water." This can be very problematic, as most sales today are from CDs and digital downloads. However, this contract at least provides that you will be paid the full Album royalty rates for digital Singles. It can also be argued that the application of this provision to digital downloads is particularly unfair considering the fact that the manufacturing, packaging and distribution costs of delivering a download to market is minimal. This contract provides that the Artist's royalties shall be calculated in the same manner and basis as the Production Companies royalties from the Distribution Company are computed, including packaging, free good and other types of deductions usually made from the retail price. The royalties will be inclusive of any royalties paid to producers of the masters and will only be paid after the Production Company has recouped all advances made to or on behalf of the Artist pursuant to the terms of the Agreement. The royalty rate is applied to the royalty base price less the container charge, which is a standard deduction based on a

CONTRACT

as to which Company is paid a percentage of net receipts, net monies or the like, Company shall credit your royalty account with an amount equal to your proportionate share of Company's receipts in connection therewith (i.e., based on the ratio of basic royalty rates for the Album from which the applicable Master is derived).

(d) Your royalty shall be calculated and computed in the same manner and on the same basis (e.g. definition of retail list price, packaging and other deductions, "free goods", other non-royalty-bearing records, etc.) as Company's royalties are calculated and computed pursuant to the Distribution Agreement. Company acknowledges that it shall furnish to Artist copies of the relevant provisions of the Distribution Agreement relating to the above promptly following Company's execution of the Distribution Agreement..

(e) With respect to Records embodying Masters made hereunder, together with other Masters, the royalty rate payable to you shall be computed by multiplying the royalty rate otherwise applicable by a fraction, the numerator of which is the number of Masters recorded hereunder contained thereon and the denominator of which is the total number of Masters contained on such Record.

ANALYSIS

percentage of the royalty base price. The container deduction percentages of twenty-five percent (25%) for CD's are common in contracts that still compute the royalty on the retail price. It's upsetting to know that labels take this deduction, that may amount to up to four dollars ($4.00) for a CD when the record company's actual cost of manufacturing each unit (including the containers) may not exceed sixty cents (60 cents). Unfortunately, most companies take a hard line and refuse to budge when asked to reduce these percentages. You might ask, "Is a packaging or container deduction applied to the sale of Internet downloads?" Well, believe it or not, a few years ago, when Internet sales were just beginning, some companies actually had the nerve to include provisions in their contracts taking a container deduction against the royalty base price of downloads. However, as the sale of music through this medium has grown, most companies have agreed to remove this deduction from the royalty base price. As indicated earlier, most major labels now compute the Artist's royalties on the wholesale (PPD) instead of the retail price, which eliminates the imposition of container deductions. This process is more transparent and preferred for Artists, so it would be a wise move to negotiate the royalties being paid on the PPD rather than the retail price. Paragraph 8. (g) allows the label to withhold a "reasonable portion" of your royalties as a reserve for returns. This is also a provision that may become outdated in the near future. In

CONTRACT

(f) With respect to Records embodying Masters made hereunder which embody your performances, together with the performances of another artist(s) to whom Company or the Distributor is obligated to pay royalties in respect of the sale of Records derived from such Masters, the royalty rate to be used in determining the royalties payable to you shall be computed by multiplying the royalty rate otherwise applicable thereto by a fraction, the numerator of which shall be "one" and the denominator of which shall be the total number of recording artists (including you) whose performance are embodied on such Master. Company and Distributor shall not require you to perform with another royalty artist.

(g) Company shall have the right to withhold a reasonable portion of your royalties as a reserve for returns, rebates, credits and exchanges. The reserve established by Company, and the liquidation thereof, shall be consistent with and not exceed the Distributor's customary policy for artists signed directly to the Distributor.

(h) If Company's royalties are computed pursuant to any Distribution Agreement on the basis of the wholesale price of Records, then the basic royalty rates hereunder shall be deemed to be adjusted so that you shall be paid or credited with the same net amounts as you

ANALYSIS

the physical distribution world, labels allow retailers to return unsold copies of records for credit to be used in purchasing other records. Some companies hold up to 50% of a new artist's royalties in reserve. Most Distribution companies agree to liquidate (pay-out earned reserved royalties) over the course of two years, a time in which the number of actual sales of albums shipped can be determined. As the digital age evolves, there will be no need for such reserves as digital copies are only downloaded upon sale and there is no return mechanism or policy allowed once the copy is sold. However, in the near future, it would be wise to impose some limitations (i.e. not in excess of 20% for Albums) on the amount of the reserves for physical products like CDs and Vinyl.

CONTRACT

would have been paid or credited hereunder.

(i) The royalty payable to you hereunder includes all royalties due you and any other Person engaged by you or engaged by Company on your behalf or deriving rights from you. You shall not be entitled to any additional compensation as the producer or co-producer of any Masters unless Company agrees in writing.

(j) No royalties shall be payable to you (or credited to your account) in respect of Phonograph Records sold by Company, the Distributor or their Licensees until payment for such Records has been received by (or credited to) Company in the United States. For accounting purposes, sales of Records hereunder by any Person other than Company (e.g., the Distributor or Company's Licensees) shall be deemed to occur in the same semi-annual accounting period in which such Person accounts to Company therefor.

9. ROYALTY ACCOUNTINGS

(a) Company shall compute royalties payable to you hereunder and will render a statement and pay such royalties, less any unrecouped Advances and any other permissible offsets within forty-five (45) days after Company receives applicable statements and payments from the Distributor in the United States. Company shall have the absolute

ANALYSIS

9. This paragraph answers the important question of when the Production Company will account to you for the royalties you earn. Most labels send accountings of royalties owed to Production Companies on a half-yearly basis (usually 60 to 90 days following June 30th and December 31st of each year.) As the Production Company needs time to calculate the Artist's portion of the royalties they receive from the Distribution Company, they

CONTRACT

right in accounting to you to rely upon the statements received by Company from the Distributor and Company shall not be responsible in any manner for any error, omission or other inaccuracy of any such statement. Company shall, simultaneously with the rendering of each royalty statement to you, send you a copy of the relevant portions of the applicable royalty statements received by Company from the Distributor. Company may deduct from any royalty (excluding mechanical royalties) or other payment due to you under this Agreement any amount you may owe Company under this Agreement. Notwithstanding the foregoing, Company shall use best efforts to cause Distributor to account and pay royalties directly to you.

(b) Royalties for Records sold for distribution outside of the United States of America (the "foreign sales") shall be computed in the national currency in which Company is paid by its Licensees and shall be paid to you at the same rate of exchanges at which Company is paid. For accounting purposes, foreign sales shall be deemed to occur in the same semi-annual accounting periods in which Company's Licensees account to Company therefor. If Company is unable, for reasons beyond its control, to receive payment for such sales in United States Dollars in the United States of America, royalties therefor shall not be credited to your

ANALYSIS

usually ask for an additional period of time to do so. This contract provides for the Artist to receive their accounting forty-five (45) days after the Production Company's receipt of their royalty statements from the Distribution Company. An artist may seek to shorten that period to thirty (30) days or less. As an example, if the Distribution Company accounted to the Production Company on September 30th and March 31st of each year, the artist could expect to receive their accounting from the Production Company on November 15th and May 15th of each year. The Production Company may deduct (recoup) from the royalties any amounts (excluding mechanical royalties) owed by the Artist to the Production Company. Including the language "excluding mechanical royalties" is very important to the Artist. If the Artist is a songwriter and writes their own material that is embodied on the recordings, the Production/Distribution Company must pay mechanical royalties (currently 9.1 cents per copy) to the Artist/songwriter for the right to use the song on the recording. As this contract also includes a provision requiring the Artist to enter into a Co-publishing agreement with the Production Company, the company could withhold the payment of mechanical royalties due the Artist to the extent that the Artist's record royalty account is unrecouped (cross-collateralize the mechanical royalties against the record royalties) and that is a bad thing. However, most companies will do as this Production Company did and not cross-collateralize

CONTRACT

account during the continuance of such inability; if any accounting rendered to you hereunder during the continuance of such inability requires the payment of royalties to you, Company will, at your request and if Company is able to do so, deposit such royalties to your credit in such foreign currency in a foreign depository, at your expense.

(c) (i) At any time within two (2) years after any royalty statement is rendered to you hereunder, you shall have the right to give Company written notice of your intention to examine Company's books and records with respect to such statement. Such examination shall be commenced within three (3) months after the date of such notice, at your sole cost and expense, by any certified public accountant or attorney designated by you, provided he is not then engaged in an outstanding examination of Company's books and records on behalf of a person other than you. Such examination shall be made during Company's usual business hours at the place where Company maintains the books and records which relate to you and which are necessary to verify the accuracy of the statement or statements specified in your notice to Company and your examination shall be limited to the foregoing. Your right to inspect Company's books and records shall be only as set forth in this Paragraph 9(c) and Company shall have no obligation to produce such books and records

ANALYSIS

the Artist's mechanical royalties against their record royalties. This paragraph also deals with the Artist's right to check or audit the Production Company's books and records to verify the accuracy of the accounting statements. This paragraph limits the period of time required for the Artist to request an audit of the Production Company's books and/or sue the Production for failing to provide an accurate accounting to three (3) years, a period of time that is dictated by California law. Under that law, regardless of what is written in an Artist agreement, an artist has the right to: 1.) request an audit and/or sue within three (3) years after the end of a royalty earnings period; 2.) retain a qualified royalty auditor (not necessarily a certified public accountant) of his/her choice, and 3.) hire an auditor who may conduct individual audits of a label's books on behalf of different artists simultaneously. Unfortunately many agreements try to limit such audit periods to two (2) years. But, no matter what this paragraph states, if the Artist or Production Company are subject to the jurisdiction of the state of California, the Artist has the aforementioned three (3) year period to conduct an audit of the Production Company's books and records.

CONTRACT

more than once with respect to each statement rendered to you.

(ii) Notwithstanding the second sentence of paragraph 9(c)(i), if Company notifies you that the representative designated by you to conduct an examination of Company's books and records under paragraph 9(c)(i) is engaged in an examination on behalf of another person ("Other Examination"), you may nevertheless have your examination conducted by your designee, and the running of the time within which such examination may be made shall be suspended until your designee has completed the Other Examination, subject to the following conditions:

(iii) You shall notify Company of your election to that effect within fifteen (15) days after the date of Company's said notice to you;

(iv) Your examination shall not be commenced by your designee before the delivery to Company of the final report on the Other Examination, shall be commenced within thirty (30) days thereafter, and shall be conducted in a reasonably continuous manner.

(d) Unless notice shall have been given to Company as provided in Paragraph 9(c) hereof, each royalty statement rendered to you shall be final, conclusive and binding on you and shall constitute an account stated. You shall be

ANALYSIS

CONTRACT

foreclosed from maintaining any action, claim or proceeding against Company in any forum or tribunal with respect to any statement or accounting rendered hereunder unless such action, claim or proceeding is commenced against Company in a court of competent jurisdiction within three (3) years after the date such statement or accountings rendered.

(e) You acknowledge that Company's books and records contain confidential trade information. Neither you nor your representatives will communicate to others or use on behalf of any other person any facts or information obtained as a result of such examination of Company's books and records.

10. WARRANTIES. REPRESENTATIONS. RESTRICTIONS AND INDEMNITIES

(a) You warrant and represent that:

(i) You are under no disability, restriction or prohibition, whether contractual or otherwise, with respect to:

(A) your right to enter into this Agreement, and

(B) your right to grant the rights granted to Company hereunder, to perform each and

ANALYSIS

10. The Production Company requires the Artist to guarantee, among other things: 1) that it has the right to enter the agreement free and clear; 2) is a member of the appropriate labor organization (union) required for them to render their services. The two primary unions for musical performers are the American Federation of Musicians (AF of M) and the American Federation of Television and Radio Artists/Screen Actors Guild (AFTRA/SAG). Both unions offer valuable services and benefits (including health insurance and pension payments) to their qualifying members. Instrumentalists join AFM and vocalists/screen actors are the primary members of AFTRA/SAG; 3) the Artist is not bound to another contract

CONTRACT

every term and provision hereof, and to record each and every Composition hereunder;

(ii) Company shall not be required to make any payments of any nature for, or in connection with, the acquisition, exercise or exploitation of rights by Company pursuant to this Agreement, except as specifically provided in this Agreement;

(iii) You are, or will become and will remain to the extent necessary to enable the performance of this Agreement, a member in good standing of all labor unions or guilds, membership in which may be lawfully required for the performance of your services hereunder;

(iv) Neither the "Materials" nor any use of the Materials by Company will violate or infringe upon the rights of any Person. "Materials" as used in this subparagraph means any musical, artistic and literary materials, ideas and other intellectual properties, furnished by you and contained in or used in connection with any recordings made hereunder or the packaging, sale distribution, advertising, publicizing or other exploitation thereof;

(v) There are not in existence any prior recorded performances by you unreleased within the United States of America and elsewhere in the world with the exclusion of mix-tape recordings, and;

ANALYSIS

that will interfere with this one; 4) the masters will not infringe on the rights of another person; 5) there are no unreleased prior recordings (other than mix-tapes, which have become the rage since the beginning of this century. You may ask who has the right to register, maintain and control the Artist's Web site? The answer under this contract is the Production Company. These types of provisions have become one of the most important provisions in recording agreements as the scope of the influence of the Internet has broadened significantly. Under the terms of this provision the Production Company is granted the right to establish, maintain, and exclusively control the Artist's official website during the term and on a non-exclusive basis after the agreement. As the value of controlling a website is increasing, these are very significant rights for artists give up. Some website business models are based on the generation of revenue from selling advertising on the site. You may note that nothing in this agreement obligates the Production Company to share any income generated from this increasingly valuable source of revenue. That is the reason these types of provisions are becoming one of the most important parts of a recording agreement. The Artist also agrees not to record any song recorded hereunder for a period of five (5) years after the release of a record containing the song or two (2) years after the expiration of this agreement, whichever is later. This provision is called a re-recording provision. Several artists have had to wait until

CONTRACT

(vi) All of your representations and warranties shall be true and correct upon execution hereof and upon delivery of each Master Recording hereunder, and shall remain in effect in perpetuity. Company's acceptance of Master Recordings or other materials hereunder shall not constitute a waiver of any of your representations, warranties or agreements in respect thereof.

(vii) Company shall have the exclusive right throughout the world during the Term and shall have the exclusive right to, for purposes of advertising, promotion and trade and in connection with the marketing and exploitation of Masters hereunder and general goodwill advertising, to authorize other Persons, to create, maintain and host any and all websites relating to the Artist and to register and use the name 'Svww.bach.com" and any variations thereof which embody the Artist's name as Uniform Resource Locators (or "URL's") addresses or domain names for each website created by Company in respect of the Artist (each, an "Artist Site"). All such websites (and related Website Material) and all rights thereto and derived therefrom shall be Company's property throughout the Territory during the Term and in perpetuity but non-exclusive thereafter. Notwithstanding the foregoing, Artist shall have the right during the Term to create, maintain and host a website for informational purposes only.

ANALYSIS

the re-recording restriction has expired to re-record some of their hit songs. Prince is an example. As the year 2000 approached, he was able to re-record his 1980's hit, "1999" to take advantage of the new millennium hype and profit from the sale of this new version on his own label. This provision also indicates that the Artist will indemnify (reimburse) the Production/Distribution Company from any claims, damages or liabilities that may arise out of any alleged breach of the aforementioned warranties (guarantees) and that the Artist agrees to provide the Production Company with any approvals it may need to effectuate the agreement, including a letter of inducement in connection with such an agreement. A letter of inducement is one written from the Artist to the Distribution Company verifying to the Distribution Company that a valid recording agreement exists between the Artist and the Production Company and that the Artist guarantees to perform their services thereunder.

| CONTRACT | ANALYSIS |

(b) (i) During the Term of this Agreement, you will not enter into any agreement which would interfere with, the full and prompt performance of your obligations hereunder, and you will not perform or render any services for the purpose of making Phonograph Records or Master Recordings for any person other than Company, except that you shall be entitled to perform as a non-featured sideman (or as otherwise allowed hereunder) in accordance with the terms and conditions of Distributor's sideman (or other applicable) clause in its agreement with Company and provided your sideman (or other applicable) performance does not materially interfere with your obligations hereunder. After the expiration of the Term of this Agreement, for any reason whatsoever, you will not perform any Composition which shall have been recorded hereunder for any person other than Company for the purpose of making Phonograph Records or Master Recordings prior to the date five (5) years subsequent to the date of delivery of the Master containing such composition or two (2) years, subsequent to the expiration date of the Term of this Agreement, whichever is later; and

(ii) You will not at any time record, manufacture, distribute or sell, or authorize or knowingly permit your performances to be recorded by any party for any purpose without an express written

CONTRACT

agreement prohibiting the use of such recording on Phonograph Records in violation of the foregoing restrictions. Notwithstanding the foregoing, Artist shall have the right to render services as a producer to third parties so long as such services do not interfere with Artist's obligations hereunder.

(iii) You shall comply with any other restriction, and shall grant any additional rights, as may be required by the Distributor pursuant to the Distribution Agreement and of which Company advises you in writing.

(c) In the event that you shall become aware of any unauthorized recording, manufacture, distribution or sale by any third party contrary to the foregoing re-recording restrictions, you shall notify Company thereof and shall cooperate with Company in the event that Company commences any action or proceeding against such third party.

(d) You will at all times indemnify and hold harmless Company and any Licensee of Company from and against any and all third party claims, damages, liabilities, costs and expenses, including legal expenses and reasonable counsel fees, arising out of any alleged breach or breach by you of any warranty, representation or agreement made by you herein which is reduced to a final judgment against Company in a court of competent jurisdiction or

ANALYSIS

CONTRACT

has been settled with your written consent. You will reimburse Company and/or Distributor on demand for any payment made at any time after the date hereof in respect of any liability or claim in respect of which Company or Distributor are entitled to be indemnified hereunder. Upon the making or filing of any such claim, action or demand, Company shall be entitled to withhold from any amounts payable under this Agreement such amounts as are reasonably related to the potential liability in issue. You may elect to post a bond in an amount and form subject to Company's reasonable approval, and in such event, Company will not so withhold monies otherwise payable to you. Company shall cease withholding monies with respect to a particular claim if no lawsuit has been commenced and the claim is not the subject of active settlement negotiations as of the date one (1) year after the claim is first made. You shall be notified of any such claim, action or demand and shall have the right, at your own expense, to participate in the defense thereof, with counsel of your own choosing; provided, however, that Company's decision in connection with the defense of any claim, action or demand shall be final.

(e) You shall execute and deliver to Company, upon Company's request therefor, a form of artist inducement and guarantee letter as may be required by a Distributor. If you shall fail or refuse to execute

ANALYSIS

CONTRACT

and deliver any such inducement letter within five (5) business days following Company's request therefor, you hereby appoint Company your true and lawful attorney-in-fact solely to execute such inducement letter in your name and on your behalf. Such power of attorney is irrevocable and is coupled with an interest and is expressly limited to an inducement letter required by Distributor from Artist.

(f) Subject to the terms hereof, you shall comply with all of the terms and conditions of this Agreement and the Distribution Agreement so that Company may perform and fulfill all of its obligations under the Distribution Agreement. You shall be provided with the relevant portions of the Distribution Agreement to which you are being required to comply.

11. DEFINITIONS

As used in this Agreement, the following terms shall have the meanings set forth below:

(a) "Master Recordings" or "Masters" - each and every Recording of Sound, whether or not coupled with a visual image, by any method and on any other substance or material, whether now or hereafter known, which is used or useful in the recording production and/or manufacture of Phonograph Records.

ANALYSIS

11. The definitions provision is one of the most important components of a recording agreement. Items that may be considered given in earlier sections of the contract can effectively be revised or taken away entirely in the definitions section. For instance, take the definition of the term "Masters" in sub paragraph (a). Throughout this Agreement the Artist might have thought they were providing performances for CD's and other musical products such as promotional videos. But when you look closely, you'll find this contract covers any form of recording of sound alone or sound

CONTRACT

(b) "Person" and "Party" - any individual, corporation, partnership, association or other organized group of persons or legal successors or representatives of the foregoing.

(c) "Records", "Phonograph Records" and "Recordings" - all forms of reproductions, now or hereafter known, manufactured or distributed primarily for home use, school use, juke box use, or use in means of transportation, embodying (i) sound alone; or (ii) sound coupled with visual images.

(d) "Advance(s)" - amount recoupable by Company from royalties to be paid to you or on your behalf pursuant to this Agreement. Advance(s) shall not be recoupable from mechanical royalties unless expressly permitted hereunder. Advance(s) shall be non-returnable, subject, however, to: (i) Company's rights at law in connection with your breach of contract; and (ii) the Distributor's right to return of advance(s) under the Distribution Agreement.

(e) "Composition" - a single musical composition, irrespective of length, including all spoken words and bridging passages and including a medley.

(f) "Recording Costs" - all payments to vocalists, musicians, arrangers, sketchers, conductors, orchestrators, producers,

ANALYSIS

together with visual images by any method... now or hereafter known. Does this mean that an artist such as Isaac Slade of the group The Fray, who is also the developer and creator of The Noisefloor TV show, has to have his non-musical performance in the show approved or consented to by his record company, SONY Records? Perhaps so under the terms of this contact. In the current age, Artists should want to preserve as many of their rights to perform in the visual media from any interference from their record companies, particularly in light of the trend of artists morphing from recording careers to TV, movies and other mixed media forms of entertainment. It's also important to note that Sub paragraph (j) denotes the requirements that must be met before delivery of the master recording is completed. The Production Company must receive not only the mixed and edited recordings, but also all necessary licenses and approvals from all participants in the recording project, including producers, guest artists (many of today's recordings have guest artists), and clearances for sampled material.

CONTRACT

contractors and copyists in connection with the recording of the Master Recordings made hereunder, and all union scale payments required to be made to you in connection with your recording services hereunder, together with payroll taxes, thereon, payments used on payroll to any labor organization or designee thereof, advances and/or fees to the producer of the Master Recordings (it being understood that no separate fee or advance shall be payable to you for any producing services in connection with the Master Recordings), the cost of cartage and rental of instruments for such recording sessions, studio costs, transportation costs, hotel and approved living expenses incurred in connection with the preparation and attendance of performers, the individual producers, musicians and other essential personnel at recording sessions, tape editing and their similar costs in connections with the production of the final tape master and the lacquer master, and all other costs generally and customarily recognized as recording costs in the phonograph industry.

(g) "Album" - one (1) twelve-inch, 33-1/3 rpm long playing Record, or the equivalent thereof, or two (2) or more such Records, packaged as a single unit or the equivalent.

(h) "Single" or "Single Record" - 7-inch or 12-inch Record

ANALYSIS

CONTRACT

embodying thereon not more than two (2) selections on each side.

(i) "Licensees" - includes, without limitation, any Distributor and all subsidiaries, wholly or partly owned, and other divisions of Company (or Distributor's) and any of Company's (or Distributor's) licensees.

(j) "Delivered" or "Delivery" - the actual receipt by Company of fully mixed and edited Master Recordings satisfactory to Company and ready for Company's manufacture of phonograph Records, and all necessary licenses, consents and approvals.

(k) "Controlled Composition" - a composition embodied in a Master Recording recorded or released hereunder, which Composition (i) is written or composed, in whole or in part, by you or (ii) is owned or controlled, in whole or in part, directly or indirectly, by you or by any Person in which you have a direct or indirect interest.

(l) "Distributor" - a record Company or other entity which has the right to distribute through normal retail channels phonograph recorded derived from the Master Recordings recorded hereunder pursuant to a Distribution Agreement.

(m) "Distribution Agreement" - an agreement pursuant to which

ANALYSIS

CONTRACT

Company grants to a third party the right to distribute, through normal retail channels phonograph records derived from the Master Recordings recorded hereunder and as more fully set forth in paragraph 21, below.

(n) "Mobile Material" - artwork, images, polyphonic (midi) ringtones, graphics, "wallpaper" and/or other materials (excluding Masters) transmitted to or reproduced as an accessory for an end user's mobile telephone or personal digital assistant (or other personal communication device)

(o) "Mobiletone" - a digital transmission (including without limitation by means of Download or Stream) of a Master (or portion[s] thereof) which may or may not be accompanied by Mobile Material to an end user's mobile telephone or personal digital assistant (or other personal communication device).

(p) "Video" - sight and sound Recordings that reproduce the audio performances of recording artists together with a visual image. For purposes of clarification only, all Videos are Recordings.

(q) "Website Material" - all material acquired or created for inclusion on a website (including, without limitation, Videos, photography, graphics, technology, so-called "hyperlinks".

ANALYSIS

CONTRACT

(r) In the event of any inconsistency between the aforesaid definitions and the definitions contained in the Distribution Agreement, the provisions of the Distribution Agreement shall control. Any terms defined in the Distribution Agreement which are not defined herein shall have the same meaning as in the Distribution Agreement.

12. SUSPENSION AND TERMINATION

(a) If your voice or your ability to perform as an instrumentalist becomes materially impaired, or if you fail, refuse, neglect or are unable to comply with any of your material obligations hereunder (including, without limitation, failure to timely fulfill your Minimum Recording Commitment), then, in addition to any other rights or remedies which Company may have, Company shall have the right, exercisable at any time by written notice to you: (i) to terminate this Agreement without further obligation to you as to unrecorded Master Recordings, (ii) to suspend its obligations hereunder (including, without limitation, the obligation to pay any advances payable hereunder) until such failure is cured, or (iii) to extend the then current Contract Period of the Term for the period of such default plus such additional time as is necessary so that Company shall have no less than one hundred fifty (150) days after completion of your recording commitment or the

ANALYSIS

12. If an Artist refuses or is unable to fulfill the terms of this agreement the Production Company may terminate or suspend the agreement until such time as the failure is cured. The Artist also has remedies should the Production Company fail to allow the Artist to fulfill its recording commitment. It's imperative to note the specific time limitations included in this provision, as certain notices to terminate the agreement are based on serving proper notices on either the Production Company or Artist. In this contract the Artist releases the Production Company from any liability for obligations other than those that survive the agreement (warranties, obligations to account, etc.) if the Artist exercises its right to terminate the contract. If an Artist has leverage they may be able to negotiate a "two firm" deal. In a two (or more) firm deal, the label is committed to record more than one album during a contract period and if the Production

CONTRACT

fulfillment of any other material obligation within which to exercise its option, if any, for the next following Contract Period. Notwithstanding the foregoing, Company shall not suspend the obligation to account to you and shall not suspend the obligation to make payments due you unless and only to the extent that the Distributor likewise suspends its obligations to make payments to Company.

(b) (i) If, in respect of any Contract Period of the Terms of this Agreement, Company fails, without cause, to allow you to fulfill your Minimum Recording Commitment, and if, within thirty (30) days after the expiration of such period, you shall notify Company of your desire to fulfill such Minimum Recording Commitment, then Company shall permit you to fulfill such Minimum Recording Commitment by notice to you to such effect within sixty (60) days of Company's receipt of your notice. Should Company fail to give such notice, you shall have the option within thirty (30) days after the expiration of said sixty (60) day period to give Company written notice that you wish to terminate the Term of this Agreement; on receipt by Company of such notice, the Term of this Agreement shall terminate and all parties will be deemed to have fulfilled all of their obligations hereunder, except those obligations which survive the end of the Term (e.g., warranties,

ANALYSIS

Company fails to fund the recording of the second album, the Artist may sue them for the amounts owed for the second album's production.

CONTRACT

re-recording restrictions and obligations to account and pay royalties), and except for such obligations, the Artist shall release the Company and the Distributor from any claims and liabilities to the Artist. In the event you fail to give Company either notice within the period specified therefor, Company shall be under no obligation to you for failing to permit you to fulfill such minimum Recording Commitment or otherwise.

(ii) Notwithstanding the foregoing, if the procedures which Company is required to follow in order to exercise an option under a Distribution Agreement corresponding to this subparagraph 12(b)(i) differ from those which you must follow in order to exercise your rights under this subparagraph 12(b)(i), then those procedures shall be substituted for those set forth herein except that any time period in which you must request Company to allow you to record as a condition for your exercise of rights in connection with Company's failure to allow you to do so shall expire fifteen (IS) days prior to the scheduled expiration of the corresponding time period under the Distribution Agreement.

(c) If, because of an act of God, inevitable accident, fire, lockout, strike or other labor dispute, riot or civil commotion, act of public enemy, enactment, rule, order or act of any government or governmental

ANALYSIS

CONTRACT

instrumentality (whether federal, state, local or foreign), failure of technical facilities, failure or delay of transportation facilities, illness or incapacity of any performer or producer, or other cause of a similar or different nature not reasonably within Distributor's or Company's control, Company or Distributor is materially hampered in the recording, manufacture, distribution or sale of Records, or Company's or Distributor's normal business operations become commercially impractical, then, without limiting Company's rights, Company shall have the option by giving you written notice to suspend the Term of this Agreement for the duration of any such contingency plus such additional time as is necessary so that Company shall have no less than thirty (30) days after the cessation of such contingency in which to exercise its option, if any, for the next following option period. Any such extension of the then-current contract year due to any change set forth in this paragraph 12(c) which involves only Company shall be limited to a period of six (6) months.

13. MECHANICAL LICENSES

(a) The mechanical licenses for compositions recorded hereunder which are written, owned or controlled, in whole or in part, by you or any entity owned or controlled by, or affiliated with you ("Controlled Compositions") are hereby licensed to Company for the United

ANALYSIS

13. In order for the Production Company and/or Distribution Company to sell a recorded version of a composition, it must get permission in the form of a license from the owner of the copyright of the composition. Usually the owner of the copyright is the publisher who obtains the rights from a songwriter or author of the composition by way of a contract or transfer of

CONTRACT

States at a rate (the "Controlled Composition Rate") equal to three-fourths (3/4) of the minimum statutory copyright royalty rate, determined as of the date the Masters were initially delivered; and for Canada at a rate equal to three-fourths (3/4) of the minimum compulsory rate in Canada (but not less than 2 cents), determined as of the date the Masters were initially delivered. Mechanical royalties shall only be payable on records for which royalties are payable hereunder. The mechanical royalty rate for any budget or mid-priced record, for any multiple-record set, and for any record sold through a record club shall be three-fourths of the Controlled Composition Rate.

(b) Notwithstanding the foregoing, the maximum rate which Company shall be required to pay in respect of an album shall be equal to ten (10) times the Controlled Composition rate, and the maximum rate in respect of any other record shall be equal to the number of compositions contained thereon (not to exceed three (3) times the Controlled Composition rate). If a 12-inch Single released by Company contains more than one (1) recording of the same Controlled Composition, Company shall not be obligated to pay the above rate more than once in respect of such Controlled Composition on such recorded. Without limiting Company's rights, you agree to indemnify and hold

ANALYSIS

rights. The publisher's job is to exploit the songwriter's compositions in exchange for fifty percent (50%) of the proceeds. In the Copyright Principles section of the book, I'll explore more fully the relationship of the publisher and the songwriter. For now let's limit the analysis to the instance where the Artist is also a songwriter. The license the Production Company must obtain is called a mechanical license. This license gives the Production and Distribution Company the right to mechanically reproduce the composition on a recording (i.e. Single, Album on CD, Vinyl or digital download). In order to simplify obtaining such a license, the U.S. copyright royalty court has set a standard royalty for licensing of the mechanical right called the compulsory minimum statutory mechanical royalty rate that is, at the time of publishing of this edition of the book, 9.1 cents or 1.75 cents per minute for songs longer than five minutes, per mechanical reproduction of the composition. This means that for the each mechanical reproduction, be it Vinyl, CD or digital download, the Production or Distribution Company must pay the copyright owner 9.1 cents for each of their compositions contained on the configuration unless agreed otherwise. Due to its investment in recording the Artist, most Production Company new artist contracts will require that any compositions written and/or controlled by the Artist be licensed to the Production Company for seventy-five percent (75%) of the compulsory minimum statutory mechanical royalty rate. In

CONTRACT

Company harmless for the payment of mechanical royalties in excess of the applicable amounts in the provisions of this paragraph 12 (and the corresponding provisions of the Distribution Agreement). If Company pays or is charged by the Distributor for any such excess, Company may recover such excess from royalties or any other payments due you hereunder.

(c) If any compositions are recorded which are not controlled Compositions, you warrant and represent that Company shall be able to obtain mechanical licenses therefor for the United States at rates and on terms no less favorable to Company than those contained in the then-current standard license form then being utilized by the Harry Fox Agency, Inc.

(d) Company is hereby granted a royalty-free license to reproduce Controlled Compositions which are embodied on Masters produced hereunder in synchronization with and in time relation to visual images featuring Artist's performances in so-called "video programs" solely for promotional usage. Commercial usage shall be negotiated in good faith.

(e) Notwithstanding anything to the contrary contained herein, Company (or Company's designee) will pay mechanical royalties at the same rates, and on the same terms and conditions (including, without

ANALYSIS

other words, for a composition controlled by the Artist, the Production Company will pay the copyright owner seventy-five percent (75%) of 9.1 cents or roughly, 6.8 cents per mechanical reproduction. While the seventy-five percent (75%) rate (sometimes referred to as the three-quarter rate) is universally objected to by many artist attorneys and publishers, most record companies strictly adhere to a policy requiring its inclusion in most new (and some established) artist contracts. Most Production/Distribution Companies also place a limit on the total amount of mechanical royalties they have to pay for specific product configurations (Single, Album, EP) and require that if the limit is exceeded the excess royalties they have to pay will be deducted from the mechanical royalties due the Artist. Many production/distribution companies limit the maximum aggregate mechanical royalties they have to pay for an album to ten times the three-quarter rate or approximately 68 cents per album. Suppose an artist's album contains 12 compositions, seven of which were composed by the Artist and five of which were written by third-party songwriters who insist upon being paid the full compulsory minimum statutory mechanical royalty rate, instead of the three-quarter rate for their compositions. In such a case, the total mechanical royalties owed by the production/distribution company would be approximately 93 cents per album or 25 cents in excess of the maximum limit. Consequently, the Artist's mechanical royalties will be

CONTRACT

limitation, aggregate maximum limitations, number of units on which mechanical royalties are paid, reserves, etc.), as are contained in the mechanical royalty provisions of the applicable Distribution Agreement. You shall also comply with the other provisions of the "Controlled Composition" provisions of the Distribution Agreement (including, without limitation, those relating to the use of musical compositions in "music videos"). You shall not be required to grant mechanical licenses for USNRC Net Sales of full price Album at less than seventy-five (75%) percent of the minimum statutory license rate as of the date of recording of the applicable Master, subject to those provisions of the Distribution Agreement relating to mechanical royalty "caps" or "overages".

14. LEGAL AND EQUITABLE RELIEF

You acknowledge that your services hereunder, as well as the Master Recordings recorded and the rights and privileges granted to Company under the terms hereof, are of a special, unique, unusual, extraordinary and intellectual character which gives them a peculiar value, and that, in the event of a breach by you of any material term, condition, representation, warranty or covenant contained herein, Company will be caused irreparable injury and damage. You expressly agree that Company shall be entitled to seek

ANALYSIS

reduced by such excess or 25 cents per album, resulting in the Artist receiving 43 cents instead of 68 cents in mechanical royalties from the sale of each album. In other words, the Production/Distribution Company is getting to include some of the Artist's compositions on the album for free. My advice to artists who have these types of provisions in their contract is to allow only ten compositions on the album if that's all you're going to be paid for and make sure all compositions written by third-party songwriters are made subject to the three-quarter rate provisions of the contract.

14. In this paragraph the Artist acknowledges that his/her services are unique and of a special character which establishes the Production Company's basis to prevent the artist from performing for another label after a mere allegation of a breach of the agreement. If the Artist fails to perform for the Production Company and attempts to provide its services to another company, the Production Company has the right to go to court and try to prevent the Artist from doing so.

CONTRACT

the remedies of injunction and other equitable relief to prevent or remedy a breach of this Agreement, which relief shall be in addition to any other rights or remedies, for damages or otherwise, which Company may have.

15. ASSIGNMENT

Company may assign this Agreement to a Distributor or to any third party or to any subsidiary, affiliated or controlling corporation or to any Person owning or acquiring a substantial portion of the stock or assets of Company. Company may also assign its rights hereunder to any of its Licensees to the extent necessary or advisable in Company's sole discretion to implement the license granted. Company shall remain primarily liable to you for its obligations hereunder unless such assignment is made to Distributor. You may not assign this Agreement or any of your rights hereunder (except to a "loan-out" corporation furnishing your services) and any such purported assignment shall be void.

16. NOTICES

Except as otherwise specifically provided herein, all notice hereunder shall be writing and shall be given by registered or certified mail or telegraph (prepaid), at the respective addresses hereinabove set forth, or such other addresses as may be designated by either party.

ANALYSIS

CONTRACT

Such notice shall be deemed given when mailed or delivered to a telegraph office, except that notice or change of address shall be effective only from the date of its receipt. A copy of all notices to Company shall be sent to Company at the address above-mentioned. A courtesy copy shall be sent to: _____
_____. A copy of all notices to Artist shall be sent to Artist at the address above-mentioned. The failure by either party to send any such courtesy copies shall not be deemed to constitute a breach hereof or to affect the validity of the notice concerned.

17. FAILURE OF PERFORMANCE

The failure by Company to perform any of its obligations hereunder shall not be deemed a breach of this Agreement unless you give Company written notice of such failure to perform and such failure is not corrected within thirty (30) days from and after Company's receipt of such notice, or, if such breach is not reasonably capable of being cured within such thirty (30) day period, Company does not commence to cure such breach within such thirty (30) day period and proceed with reasonable diligence to complete the curing of such breach thereafter.

18. NAME AND LIKENESS; MERCHANDISING: TOURING: ADDITIONAL ACTIVITIES

ANALYSIS

18. This paragraph is the first of three that effectuate the 360° (All-rights) nature of this agreement. The All-rights type of deal unfortunately (in

CONTRACT

(a) Company shall have the perpetual right (such right to be exclusive during the Term and non-exclusive thereafter), without any liability to any party, to use and to authorize others to use your name and approved biographical material and the names (including any professional names heretofore or hereafter adopted), and any approved photographs or likenesses, autographs and biographical material relating to Artist and any producer of Masters hereunder for purposes of advertising, promotion and trade and in connection with the making and exploitation of Masters, Recordings and Records hereunder and in connection with the creation and exploitation of merchandise and in general goodwill advertising. You warrant and represent that you own the exclusive right to so use such names, likenesses, autographs (including facsimile signatures) and biographical materials and that the use of same will not infringe upon the rights of any third party. If any third party challenges your right to use a professional name, Company may, at its election and without limiting Company's rights, require you to adopt another professional name approved by Company without awaiting the determination of the validity of such challenge. During the Term, you will not change the name by which you are professionally known without Company's prior written approval.

ANALYSIS

the opinion of many artist attorneys), have become the norm in the record business. All-rights agreements enable the record and/or production companies to participate in the earnings from every source of an artist's career. Most major and many independent labels have insisted on signing new artists to 360 deals since sales of recorded product started to rapidly decline after the beginning of this century. Please see the section on 360 Deals for more information on the history and impact of this, now standard, method of exploiting an artist's talent. First, the language in this paragraph give the Production Company rights to exploit the Artist's name, photos and likenesses in any manner of merchandising ventures. The Artist should try to limit the use of these rights to activities that have received their prior consent. In addition, while the Production Company agrees to pay the Artist fifty percent (50%) of the proceeds generated from the exploitation of these rights, any royalties the Artist is entitled to are applied to the Artist royalty account. In other words, merchandising royalties are cross-collateralized against the Artist record royalty account. That isn't a good thing. You should always try to avoid cross-collateralization at all costs. If an artist has any leverage they may be able to negotiate separate royalty accounts for record, video, merchandising and publishing royalties. That's important because, in most cases, the artist royalty account is usually in an unrecouped position. Whereas, if an artist has a great image

CONTRACT

(b) The name, likeness and merchandising rights granted to Company pursuant to subparagraph 18(a) above include the exclusive right during the Term hereof and throughout the Territory for Company to use and/or sublicense to others the use of your name(s) (both real and professional), logotype, photographs, likenesses and facsimile signature(s) for merchandising and other commercial purposes (whether or not such merchandising and commercial purposes are related to the manufacture and sale of Records) in connection with the sale of merchandise, including without limitation, t-shirts, shirts, sweatshirts and other clothing and apparel, posters, stickers, novelties, dolls, action figures, figurines, games, video games, ring-tones, all paper products, Internet uses, and for any and all other so-called "merchandising" uses. Subject to your full performance of all of Your obligations hereunder, Company will credit to Your royalty account hereunder Fifty (50%) percent of Company's "Net Merchandise Income" from the exploitation of such rights and Company shall retain the remaining Fifty (50%) percent of such Net Merchandise Income for its own account. "Net Merchandise Income" shall mean the income actually received by Company from the exploitation of merchandising rights relating to you less all costs and expenses incurred by Company, directly or

ANALYSIS

and sells a lot of merchandise, the merchandise royalty account may recoup and start generating income for the Artist sooner. In addition to merchandising, this paragraph allows the Production Company to participate in touring monies at a rate of twenty percent (20%) of the "gross touring income." Most companies only passively participate in this area, in that they don't really take steps to arrange touring dates and activities. They only get their "cut" . . . in this case 20%. Some companies will either reduce the percentage (normal ranges are 10-20%), or agree to take their percentage on the "net" income (i.e. gross income less expenses). Sometimes an artist may only net 30% of the gross touring income after paying the costs of travel, lodging, side-musicians, crew, managers and agents fees. So, you can see why its better for the Artist to pay the Production Company fees based on net rather than the gross touring income. Pursuant to this paragraph, the Production Company is also engaged as the Artist's personal manager. For providing these services the company gets paid a 20% commission on the Artist's gross income. In my estimation this provision is over-reaching and should be negotiated very carefully. First, the Artist should insist that touring income is excluded from the definition of gross income subject to a manager commission, as the Production already requests 20% of gross touring income. Secondly, publishing revenues should also be excluded. As you will read in the very next paragraph, the Production Company

CONTRACT

indirectly, relating to the exploitation of such rights. After the expiration or termination of the Term, Company's merchandise rights shall continue in perpetuity with respect to merchandise products or services created or exploited during the Term.

(c) You shall pay Company (or to whom Company directs) a fee equal to Twenty (20%) percent of the "Gross Touring Income" derived as a result of your "live" personal appearance performance engagements ("Live Performance(s)") which are performed during the Term (or within six (6) months thereafter). Company's said fee shall be payable to Company within thirty (30) days after receipt by you, directly or indirectly, or by any Person on your behalf, of the Gross Touring Income upon which such fee is based. For purposes of this subparagraph 11(c), "Gross Touring Income" shall mean all monies and other consideration earned by you or your behalf, or which is committed to be paid to you, directly or indirectly, in connection with any Live Performance(s). It is expressly understood and agreed that Company is neither an employment agency, a talent or theatrical agency nor a booking agent, and that Company has not offered or promised to obtain employment or engagements for you, and that Company is not obligated, authorized or expected to do so.

ANALYSIS

insists that the Artist also enter into a Co-publishing agreement with their publishing company. These types of provisions are rife with possibilities of conflict of interest claims by the Artist, as the Production Company may not be inclined to represent the best interests of the Artist in any negotiations for increased advances or royalty payments with their affiliated production or publishing divisions. The language of Paragraph 18. (g) seems to acknowledge that fact by insisting the Artist waive any claims of conflict of interest and agree that the Artist attorney, not the Production Company, will conduct negotiation of material terms of agreements on behalf of the Artist.

CONTRACT

(d) In addition to the rights of Company as set forth herein (and without limiting same), you hereby engage Company on a non-exclusive basis during the Term and throughout the universe, to represent you as your exclusive Personal Manager in connection with all of your services, activities and undertakings throughout the entertainment industry, including, but not limited to, your services as a producer of sound recordings, songwriter, musical composer, publisher, live performer, actor, screenwriter, producer of audio-visual works, director, model, spokesperson, and all other performances and activities throughout all fields of the entertainment industry, including, without limitation, in the fields of music, recording, television, motion pictures, radio, Internet, and any and all public performances, and in connection with merchandise endorsements, commercials and any and all other exploitations of your services, talents and activities in any way connected with or appurtenant to the entertainment industry and related fields throughout the universe (individually and collectively, "Entertainment Services"). Artist shall not appoint any other person or entity to provide personal management services to Artist during the Term.

(e) In the event that Company (or its agents) or third-parties (i.e., Agents, etc.) secure any

ANALYSIS

CONTRACT	ANALYSIS
opportunities or proposed agreements which you accept at any time during the Term or within twelve (12) months thereafter (individually and collectively, "Covered Agreement(s)"), you agree that Company shall be entitled to receive a commission ("Commission") in connection with all such Covered Agreements. The rate of Company's Commission shall be equal to Twenty (20%) percent of all "Gross Income" (as hereinafter defined in this paragraph) derived as a result of all Covered Agreements and all Entertainment Services which are performed and/or rendered by you at any time pursuant to any Covered Agreements, as well as all extensions, renewals and modifications thereof (or replacements therefor). It is expressly understood and agreed that notwithstanding the expiration or termination of the Term of this agreement, Company shall continue to receive its Commission hereunder in perpetuity. "Gross Income" as used in this paragraph shall mean all gross sums of money or other considerations including, but not limited to, fees, salaries, earnings, royalties, residuals, advances, union fees, bonuses, proceeds of sales, leases or licenses, recording costs, gifts, shares of stock and partnership, corporate, LLC or other interests, directly or indirectly earned or received by you or your heirs, successors and assigns, or earned or received by anyone on your behalf, in connection	

CONTRACT

with your Entertainment Services and related activities.

(f) You hereby irrevocably authorize and direct any payors of Gross Income earned pursuant to any Covered Agreements (and you shall further direct and authorize such parties (via a Letter of Direction) to the extent necessary or requested by Company) to render statements and payments directly to Company for the Commission at the same times as the monies relating to Company's Commission are payable to you. In the event that any payor fails or refuses to pay Company directly, you shall pay Company its Commission within five (5) days of your receipt thereof. You agree to furnish Company with a true and complete copy of any Covered Agreements promptly following Company's request therefor.

(g) You hereby acknowledge that _____ is the principal owner of Company and, accordingly, you hereby agree to waive any claims of conflict which may or may not arise as a result. You further acknowledge and agree that any negotiations or re-negotiations regarding the material terms of this Agreement shall be conducted by your attorney.

19. **VIDEOS**

(a) Company shall have the right to require you, upon reasonable advance notice, to perform at

ANALYSIS

19. Most artists require videos for at least two singles per album and in this day of YouTube videos for every song released, the costs of producing videos can be staggering. Simple YouTube

CONTRACT

such times and places as Company designates for the production of films or videotapes featuring your performances of Compositions embodied on Master Recordings recorded hereunder (hereinafter "Videos"). Company shall be the exclusive owner throughout the world and in perpetuity of such Videos and all rights therein, including all copyrights and renewal of copyrights, excluding the rights in and to the underlying musical compositions embodied on such Videos and shall have all of the rights with respect thereto which are set forth in Paragraph 7 above, including without limitation, the right (but not the obligation) to use and exploit such Videos in any and all forms. Notwithstanding the foregoing, Company acknowledges that Artist shall have consultation rights with respect to the creative elements of any Video produced hereunder.

(b) All sums paid by Company in connection with the production and promotion of Videos shall constitute Advances to you which are recoupable from royalties, excluding mechanical royalties, payable to you pursuant to this Agreement. All sums paid by Company's Distributor in connection with the production of Videos which are recoupable from sums under the Distribution Agreement shall be recoupable hereunder in the same manner and to the same extent that Distributor recoups such costs from Company.

ANALYSIS

videos can be recorded for less than a $1,000, but professionally produced ones can cost from $10,000 to over $100,000. Video costs have come to be considered an additional expense recoupable from an artist's record royalties that make it even more difficult for the artist to recoup. This is because usually 50% to 100% of video costs are usually recoupable from the artist's record royalties. In this contract you will notice that 100% of the video costs are recoupable from the artist's record royalties. This is an extreme position for a production/distribution company to take. Usually a production/distribution company contract will provide that only 50% of video costs (at least up to a certain dollar amount) are recoupable from record royalties. However, 100% of said costs may be recouped from royalties due the artist from commercial exploitation of the video such as DVD sales or streaming. This contract calls for the artist to receive a video royalty of 50% of the Production Company's net receipts from the exploitation of the videos. A better contract may provide for the payment of a higher royalty of 20%–30% of the gross proceeds of video sales, instead of net receipts, less a distribution fee.

CONTRACT	ANALYSIS
(c) As to the exploitation of the Videos by Company's licensees, Company shall credit your account with fifty (50%) percent of Company's net receipts attributable to the Videos. ("Net receipts" shall mean all amounts received by Company less any amount which Company pays in connection with the exploitation of the Videos, including payments to publishers, promotion personnel, labor organizations, shipping and duplication costs, and distribution fees, but not including payments to the producer of the Master Recording). Your share of Company's net receipts shall be inclusive of any compensation for the use of any Controlled Compositions contained in the Videos.	
20. CO-PUBLISHING	
(a) (i) In consideration of the mutual promises and covenants herein contained, you hereby irrevocably and absolutely assign, convey and set over to Company's music publishing designee ("Publisher"), an undivided fifty (50%) percent interest in the so-called "publisher's share" of the worldwide copyright (which represents 25% of the whole musical composition (and all renewals, extensions, continuations, reversions and restorations thereof) and all other rights in and to each Controlled Composition. (ii) For the avoidance of confusion, of every one ($1.00)	20. As indicated earlier, the Artist is also required to enter into a Co-publishing agreement with the Production Company. While the terms of the Co-publishing deal are briefly covered in this paragraph, I urge you to review the more detailed Co-publishing and Administration agreement in a later chapter that gives you a paragraph-by-paragraph analysis of the material terms of this type of deal. However, the inclusion of this paragraph in the Agreement clearly indicates the active nature of the Production Company's involvement in administering the Artist's copyrights. As you can read, the Production Company gets 25% of the gross receipts from the exploitation of the Artist's compositions. But this raises a

CONTRACT

Dollar of mechanical publishing income generated, you shall receive seventy-five (75%) percent and Company shall retain twenty-five (25%) percent. Likewise, any third-party publishing advance directly attributable to the Controlled Compositions shall be apportioned as mentioned above.

(b) (i) Publisher shall be the exclusive administrator of all rights in and to each such Controlled Composition, and it shall be entitled to exercise any and all rights with respect to the control, exploitation and administration of the Controlled Composition, including without limitation, the sole right to grant licensees, collect all income and to use the name, approved likeness and approved biographical material of each composer, lyricist and songwriter hereunder in connection with each applicable Controlled Composition for the full term of copyright (including all renewals and extensions thereof) in and to each Controlled Composition; and

(ii) Without limiting the generality of the foregoing, BMI, ASCAP or SESAC (the "Society") shall be authorized and directed to pay the publisher's share of performance of Controlled Compositions in the United States and Canada directly to Publisher.

(c) You represent and warrant that the Controlled Compositions

ANALYSIS

very interesting question: Does the Production Company collect this fee plus an additional 20% management commission on the balance of royalties earned by the Artist? Personally, I don't think the Production Company should be able to "double-dip" on the Artist's publishing earnings in this way. That is why I would negotiate to have any publishing earnings excluded from the definition of gross income subject to the manager commission. The Production Company is actively engaged in exploitation of the Artist's compositions and is entitled to its 25% of the proceeds and that should suffice.

CONTRACT

are original and do not infringe upon or violate the rights of any other person and that you have the full and unencumbered right, power and authority to grant to Publisher all of the rights herein granted to Publisher. You hereby indemnify Publisher against any loss, damage or expense (including reasonable attorney's fees) in respect of any third party claims, demands, liens or encumbrances. Publisher shall have the benefit of all warranties and representations given by the writers of the Controlled Compositions.

(d) From all royalties earned and received by Publisher in the United States of America from the exploitation of the Controlled Compositions throughout the world (the "Gross Receipts"), Publisher shall:

(i) Deduct and retain all documented out-of-pocket costs incurred by Publisher in connection with the exploitation, administration and protection of the Controlled Compositions;

(ii) Deduct and pay royalties payable to the writers of the Controlled Compositions (which you warrant and represent shall not exceed fifty (50%) percent (i.e., "the writer's share*") of the Gross Receipts) after deduction of the amounts set forth in clause (i) above and which shall not include any share of publisher's share of public performance income (i.e., the

ANALYSIS

CONTRACT

so-called "writer's share" of public performance income); and

(iii) Pay to you an amount equal to fifty (50%) percent of the balance remaining after deducting the aggregate sums set forth in subparagraphs (i) and (ii) above (i.e., the "Publisher's share"), and the remaining fifty (50%) percent thereof shall be retained by Publisher for its sole use and benefit (i.e., the "Publisher's share").

(e) Accountings for such royalties shall be rendered semi-annually subject to all the terms and provisions of paragraph 9 hereof.

(f) Any assignment made of the ownership or copyright in, or rights to license the use of, any Controlled Compositions referred to in this paragraph shall be made subject to the provisions hereof. The provisions of this paragraph are accepted by you, on your own behalf and on behalf of any other owner of any Controlled Compositions or any rights therein.

(g) You shall promptly provide Publisher with a copy of your songwriter agreement with the writer of each Controlled Composition or such other agreement evidencing your rights in and to such Controlled Composition, and you shall provide Publisher with copies of such agreements with respect to Controlled Compositions not yet created promptly after their creation.

ANALYSIS

CONTRACT

(h) You shall execute and deliver to Publisher any documents (including without limitation, assignments of copyright and Publisher's standard co-publishing agreement [subject to negotiation of the non-substantive provisions thereof]) which Publisher may require to vest in Publisher and/or its designees the copyright and other rights herein granted to Publisher in respect of each Controlled Composition. If you shall fail to execute such document within five (5) business days from your receipt of Publisher's request therefor, you hereby irrevocably grant to Publisher a limited power of attorney solely to execute such document in your name and solely with respect to the Controlled Compositions hereunder.

21. DISTRIBUTION AGREEMENT

In the event that at any time during the Term, Company shall enter into the Distribution Agreement, then, notwithstanding anything to the contrary contained in this Agreement:

(a) Company shall have the right, at Company's election, to extend any Contract Period(s) to be co-extensive plus an additional thirty (30) days;

(b) From time to time, Company shall have the unrestricted right (but not the obligation), at

ANALYSIS

CONTRACT

Company's election, to conform any provision (e.g., reserves, free goods, etc.) of this Agreement to the provision of the Distribution Agreement which comprehends the same subject matter, including, without limitation, the Term and the Minimum Recording Commitment; (subject to written notification of Artist and Artist's counsel of such matter as well as prompt provision to Artist's counsel of such documentation) however, Company shall not decrease your Advances hereunder by reason of any such conforming; and

(c) You hereby agree to duly execute any letters of inducement that may be required pursuant to the Distribution Agreement.

22. APPROVALS

Whenever in this Agreement your or Company's approval or consent is required, such approval or consent shall not be unreasonably withheld. Company shall require you to formally give or withhold such approval or consent by giving you written notice requesting same and by furnishing you with the information or material in respect of which such approval or consent is sought. You shall give Company written notice of approval or disapproval within five (5) business days after such notice. You shall not hinder or delay the scheduled release of any record hereunder. In the event of

ANALYSIS

CONTRACT

disapproval or no consent, the reasons therefor shall be stated.

23. MISCELLANEOUS

(a) This Agreement contains the entire understanding of the parties hereof relating to the subject matter hereof and cannot be changed or terminated except by an instrument signed by the party bound. A waiver by either party of any term or condition of this Agreement in any instance shall not be deemed or construed as waiver of such term of condition for the future, or of any subsequent breach thereof. All remedies, rights, undertakings, obligations, and agreements contained in this Agreement shall be cumulative and none of them shall be in limitation of any other remedy, right, undertaking, obligation or agreement of either party. The headings of the paragraphs hereof are for convenience only and shall not be deemed to limit or in any way affect the scope, meaning or intent of this Agreement or any portion thereof.

(b) It is understood and agreed that in entering into this Agreement, and in rendering services pursuant thereto, you have, and shall have, the status of an independent contractor and nothing herein contained shall contemplate or constitute you as Company's employee or agent.

ANALYSIS

CONTRACT

(c) Those provisions of any applicable collective bargaining agreement between Company and any labor organization which are required, by the terms of such agreement, to be included in this Agreement shall be deemed incorporated herein.

(d) This Agreement has been entered into the State of _____ and the validity, interpretation and legal effect of this Agreement shall be governed by the laws of the State of _____ applicable to contracts entered into and performed entirely within the State of _____. The courts, only, will have jurisdiction of any controversies regarding this Agreement; and, any action or other proceeding which involves such a controversy will be brought in the courts located within the State of _____ and not elsewhere. Any process in any action or proceeding commenced in the courts of the State of _____ arising out of any such claim, dispute or disagreement, may, among other methods, be served upon you by delivering or mailing the same, via registered or certified mail, or via a commercial carrier which provides proof of receipt, addressed to you at the address first above written or such other address as you may designate pursuant to Paragraph 15 hereof. Any such delivery or mail service shall be deemed to have the same force and effect as personal service within the State of _____.

ANALYSIS

CONTRACT

(e) If any part of this Agreement shall be determined to be invalid or unenforceable by a court of competent jurisdiction or by any other legally constituted body having jurisdiction to make such determination, the remainder of this Agreement shall remain in full force and effect.

IN WITNESS WHEREOF, the parties hereto have executed this Agreement on or about the day and year first above written.

AGREED TO AND ACCEPTED:

Company

By: _____
     An Authorized Signatory

Artist

_____

ANALYSIS

9

Statement and Analysis of Recording Earnings

Why having a Million-Seller doesn't Mean a Million Dollar$ to the Artist

When I was in junior high and high school taking math and algebra classes, I would complain (along with most of my classmates!) that we would never use in the "real world" what we were being taught in school, so what was the sense in learning it? Well, welcome to the "real world." If you want to be in this or any other business, you've got to be able to read, write, and count (as well as figure). For all of you who have talent and say you want to be in the music business, master the three R's: "Readin', 'Ritin', and 'Rithmetic," because believe me, in the real world all aspects of business are based on them.

The purpose of this analysis is to show the correlation of the accounting statements to the provisions of the contracts which give rise to them. I think this is very important because it gets to the essence of the music *business*, how the money is made. Watch, as the money the production company or the artist is entitled to either flows through or is bottled up in certain provisions of the contract.

The statement of recording earnings is based on some very important assumptions. In that our sample exclusive recording artist contract is between the production company and the artist, we must first assume that another contract exists between the production company and a major distributor for the manufacture and distribution of the artist's recordings. We must also make other assumptions regarding the production company/distributor contract that will help us complete our analysis.

The first assumption is that the production company/distributor contract provides that the major distributor will pay the production company an "all-in recording fund" of $250,000 per album and an "all-in royalty" of 15%. An "all-in" designation of a fund or royalty is an industry term describing how the monies for the recording will be disbursed and categorized by the distributor. In deals with new production companies most distributors will offer to pay the recording costs for the album under what is called a "recording budget" as opposed to the preferable "all-in recording fund" method. In a recording budget type of deal, the distributor will allow the production company to spend a predetermined maximum amount for the recording of the album, provided the costs are submitted to the distributor for direct payment on an itemized invoice basis. In this type of deal, it is necessary for the production company to account for all recording costs. If it is determined, after the album is completed, that the recording costs fall short of the approved recording budget, the distributor, not the production company, keeps the balance of the budget not expended.

However, in an "all-in recording fund" type of agreement (as in our example) the distributor pays the production company $250,000 to record the album. This amount is payable in its entirety directly to the production company, usually in installments of $125,000 upon commencement of recording of the album and the balance of $125,000 upon satisfactory delivery of the album. In exchange for the payment to the production company of the entire amount of the fund, the distributor expects, and indeed contractually requires, the production company to pay all costs associated with the recording and delivery of the master recordings comprising the album.

You might remember the advice I shared in my earlier explanation of "When a Million Dollars, Ain't a Million Bucks." While $250,000 sounds like a lot of money, keep in mind that there are definite costs associated with producing an album. In the case of a production company, the key outlay is recording costs, which include a wide range of expenses, such as payments to musicians, studio costs, equipment rental, recording artist advances, producer fees or advances and mastering fees. Sounds like a lot, right? It is, but the beauty of the all-in-recording fund arrangement is that the production company, not the distributor, gets to keep the balance of the fund if the album recording costs are less than the amount of the recording fund. When we do the math, we see that if the recording fund is $250,000 per album and the production company delivers a satisfactory album at a cost of $150,000 ($100,000 in recording costs + $50,000 artist advance), the production company gets to pocket $100,000.

An "all-in royalty" is similar to an "all-in-recording fund" in regard to its effect on the production company. You'll hear the term "*points*" used a lot in the record business. A point is one percentage (1%) point of either the retail price or wholesale price of either an album or a single. In most major label contracts the selling price is the wholesale price. In an all-in royalty type of deal, as in this instance, the production company receives a royalty of 15%, out of which the production company must pay all royalty participants they contract with to produce or perform on the record. If the artist's album royalty is twelve percent (12%), the production company will be entitled to retain for itself a royalty of three percent (3%), the balance of royalties left after deduction of the artist's royalty.

The second assumption is that this statement covers the sale of only one (1) album and two (2) singles.

The third assumption is that the other provisions of the production company/distributor contract are similar to the exclusive recording artist/production company contract, which allows the recoupment of 50% of video and independent promotion costs.

The fourth assumption is that sales for which the accounting statement is submitted included 200,000 albums (150,000 CD's and 50,000 digital copies) and 200,000 copies of single #1 and 100,000 copies of single #2. Let's first look at the advances.

Production Company			*Artist*
		Advances	
	$250,000	From Distributor	
Less	100,000	Recording Costs	
	50,000	Advance to Artist	$50,000 From Production Co.
	$100,000	Profit to Production Co.	

As I indicated in the first assumption, the production company received an "all-in-recording fund" of $250,000 for delivery of the album and two (2) singles. The recording costs are $100,000 and the artist's advance (pursuant to the exclusive recording artist/production company contract) is $50,000. Therefore, the production company keeps $100,000 of the fund. Now let's take a look at the royalties due the production company and the artist from the sale of albums and singles.

ROYALITES FROM SALES OF ALBUMS AND SINGLES

Album Sales

Production Company Royalties		Artist Royalties	
$7.50	PPD	$7.50	PPD
× 15%	Prod Co. Royalty Rate	× 12%	Artist Royalty Rate
$1.13	Royalty per Album	$ .90	Artist Royalty per Album
200,000	Albums Shipped	200,000	Albums Shipped
−40,000	Free Goods	−40,000	Free Goods
160,000	Albums Sold	160,000	Albums Sold
× $1.13	Royalty per Album	× $.90	Royalty per Album
$180,800	Total Album Royalty	$144,000	Total Album Royalty

Single Sales

$.75	PPD		$.75	PPD
× 15%	Prod. Co. Royalty Rate		× 12%	Artist Royalty Rate
$.11	Royalty per single		$.09	Royalty per Single
200,000	Single #1		200,000	Single #1
100,000	Single #2		100,000	Single #2
300,000	Total Singles		300,000	Total Singles
× $.11	Royalty Per Single		× $.09	Royalty per Single
$33,000	Total Single Royalty		$27,000	Total Single Royalty

In addition to reducing their staffs, trimming artist rosters and entering into 360 deals with artists, major record labels also made another big move in reaction to the drastic downturn in album sales. They reduced the price of their albums. At one time, in the not too distant past, some major labels calculated artist royalties on the suggested retail list price (SRLP) after taking numerous deductions for packaging, breakage, free goods and new media configurations that discounted the royalties due the artist. Now, most of the major labels compute artist royalties on the net wholesale price PPD and have eliminated some of the reductions to the artist royalty account. One major label group took the drastic step of reducing the wholesale price of CDs from $10–$12 to $7.50 or less, in an effort to increase volume sales. The label established a published suggested retail price that would allow it a 25% profit margin. So an album with a SRLP of $10 would be sold to wholesalers at a PPD of $7.50. This is a far cry from the heyday of CD sales in the nineties when a superstar artist's album may have had a SRLP of $18.98. The year after year decrease in album sales appears to be leveling off, but the change in wholesale prices has lowered profits to the labels as well as the amount of royalties due artists. As the PPD of most new artists' albums is approximately $7.50 for albums and $.75 for singles, a royalty rate of 15% means the production company receives a royalty of $1.13 per album and

$.11 per single. In the case of the artist, whose royalty rate is 12%, the royalty due per album is $.90 and $.09 per single.

Even though the majors that pay royalties on the PPD have eliminated the imposition of packaging and breakage deductions, some still impose free-goods (copies given to a store as incentive for them to buy a greater number of records) deductions. For instance, if a store agrees to buy 100 albums, the label may give them an additional 15–20 free. This, of course, lowers the per unit price by 15–20% and although some artist attorneys try to limit this deduction to CD albums only it is still prevalent for labels to take a free goods deduction for all albums sold.

In this statement of recording earnings of sales of albums and singles, the production company is getting a royalty of $1.13 per album and $.11 per single. After the 20% free goods deduction the number of royalty-bearing albums is 160,000. When you multiply that number by the per album royalty album royalty rate, it results in the production company earning $180,800 for albums and the artist being entitled to $144,000 of that amount. In regard to singles, the per single royalty rate multiplied by the number sold results in the production company earning $33,000 in single royalties with the artist receiving $27,000 of that amount.

The total royalties earned for both Album and Singles configurations would be as follows:

Production Company		*Artist*	
TOTAL ALBUM AND SINGLES ROYALTIES			
$180,800	Album Royalties	$144,000	Album Royalties
$ 33,000	Single Royalties	$ 27,000	Single Royalties
$213,800	Total Royalties	$171,000	Total Royalties

ROYALTIES FROM THIRD PARTY USES

While sales of recordings have decreased since the beginning of the century, new sources of revenue from their use have emerged and are worth noting. Third-party use of recordings in movies, TV, videos, commercials, other recordings (sampling) and Internet streaming activity is growing. Both record companies and artists are hopeful that these ancillary income streams will eventually offset the decrease in album sales. In most contracts with record companies 50% of third-party income is paid to the production company that, in turn, is responsible for paying 50% of the amount it receives to the artist. Let's take a look at a sample of these earnings.

SYNCHRONIZATION USES

One form of third-party use occurs when an audio recording is used in time-synchronization with a video image (Synchronization use). If a recording is used in a video commercial, TV program, movie, video, video Internet series, etc., the producer of such work must obtain permission from the owner of the sound recording (record company) and that permission is usually granted upon the payment of a licensing fee. The amount of synch fees vary based on the type, length, context of the use of the sound recordings and budget of the licensor. These fees can be substantial in the instance of a well-known recording. In our example we will assume that two recordings from the album have been licensed for synch uses, one in a commercial and the other in a movie. The commercial synch license use fee is $10,000 paid to the Distributor and the movie synch license fee is $20,000 paid to Distributor. Both the production company and artist are entitled to receive 50% of the net amount realized.

Production Company Royalties	*Artist Royalties*
Commercial Synch Fee	
$ 5,000.00 (50% of $10,000)	$2,500.00 (50% of $5,000)
Movie Synch Fee	
$10,000.00 (50% of $20,000)	$5,000.00 (50% of $10,000)
Total $15,000.00	$7,500.00

SAMPLING

Sampling is a third-party use that occurs when a portion of one recording is digitally inserted into a new recording. Under copyright law if a copyrighted work is used to derive a new copyrighted work, a license must be obtained to create the derivative work. This technique first became very popular during the development of Hip Hop music and is still prevalent today. When a prior audio recording is sampled into a new one, permission must be granted from the owner of the sampled recording and this, too, is usually obtained through the payment of a license fee. Let's make the assumption that another artist sampled one of the tracks on the album and the Distributor was paid a $15,000.00 license fee for the use.

Production Company Royalties	*Artist Royalties*
Sampling (Derivative Rights) fee $7,500.00 (50% of $15,000)	$3,750.00 (50% of $7,500)

IS A DIGITAL DOWNLOAD A THIRD PARTY USE?

Should a production company's royalty rate for a sale of a digital download album be paid on the same basis as a typical sale of a CD (e.g. 15%) or as a third-party license (50%)? That is a question many artists and production companies are asking. Several artists have sued their record companies arguing the latter rather than the former and, even though there has been at least one court decision agreeing that a digital download should be considered as a third-party license rather than a typical sale, most record companies still insist this type of transaction be treated as a sale rather than a license.

STREAMING

Within a few years of the turn of the new century, it was predicted the massive increase of P2P file sharing would lead to a new digital age where people would no longer yearn for ownership of a CD, vinyl or any other physical configuration of music. Instead, a new paradigm would emerge that focused on music consumers paying for the right to have access to any of the music they desire, on any device capable of streaming such music, at any time. Some looked to the development of cable TV and satellite radio as models of what could happen if tens of millions of people paid monthly subscriptions to access all the music they desired. Over one hundred million people in the U.S. pay bills, some in excess of $100 per month for the right to watch cable TV. When XM and Sirius satellite radio networks merged in 2005, the combined number of total subscribers was 14 million. Eight years later the number of subscribers paying $12.95 per month or more had increased to 25 million. These developments encouraged innovators and entrepreneurs to develop businesses that could supply consumers with all the music they desired, at any time, for a monthly subscription fee. However, initially major labels were not willing of to license their massive catalog of recordings for streaming purposes. Certain radio-like Internet services like Pandora, obtained compulsory licenses that required a royalty rate to be paid to record companies and artists for each stream. But many developing services like Spotify, iRadio and iHeartRadio negotiated directly with major labels for the right to stream their music on both a radio-like service and on-demand basis. As the second decade of the 21st century progresses, these subscription models have to prove that they can reach the scale of several tens of millions of subscribers to make the model viable. Within two years of their 2011 launch in the U.S., Spotify boasted that six million of their 24 million users were subscribers and that it paid 70% of ad revenue and subscription fees to record companies, artists, songwriters and publishers. However, several artists have complained about the low royalties they receive from these new streaming services. Streaming royalties for artists and record companies may be only fractions of a penny per stream ranging from $.001–$.003 depending on the whether the stream is from a radio-like or on-demand service. But many music insiders predict that, as these services multiply their base of ad support and subscribers, royalty payments will increase to a rate that fairly compensates music creators and record companies. SoundExchange, a non-profit performance rights organization was established by the Recording Industry Association of America (RIAA) to collect digital performance royalties on behalf of sound recording owners (record companies) and artists. Surprisingly, major labels agreed to allow SoundExchange to pay royalties on the same basis of a third-party license, e.g. dividing streaming royalties 50% to the label, 45% to the featured artist and 5% to the non-featured artist (session players) unions AFM and SAG/AFTRA. However, for artists and record companies to receive these royalties, they must register with SoundExchange. So, be sure to register so you can be paid this important new source of revenue from streaming services. If you haven't registered yet, do it now!

While these royalties may have been earned by the production company and the artist, it is not necessarily the amount payable to each of them. The amount due each party will depend upon the terms of their agreements. In the case of the production company, it will be based on its deal with the major record distributor and in the case of the artist, it's determined by the exclusive recording artist contract with the production company.

As indicated earlier, based on the assumption that the production company's contract with the major record distributor is an "all-in" deal, the production company is responsible for payment of the advances and royalties due the artist according to its exclusive recording artist contract.

Now let's take a look at a sample royalty statement for the production company and artist. Keep in mind that the distributor must account to the production company by submitting a royalty statement. The production company, in turn (according to the exclusive recording artist contract), is obligated to submit a royalty statement to the artist.

SAMPLE ROYALTY STATEMENT

Production Company Royalties	Artist Royalties
$15,000 Royalties from Synch Uses	$7,500 Royalties from Synch Uses
7,500 Royalties from Sampling	3,750 Royalties from Sampling
213,800 Royalties from Sales	171,000 Royalties from Sales
−53,450 Reserve (25% of Sales)	−42,750 Reserve (25% of Sales)
−250,000 Advance from Distributor	−150,000 Recording Cost
	−50,000 Advance from Prod. Co.
−30,000 Video Costs (50% of $60,000) (50% of $60,000)	−30,000 Video Costs
−25,000 Indie Promo Costs (50% of $50,000)	−25,000 Indie Promo Costs (50% of $50,000)
−122,150 Unrecouped Balance with Distributor	−115,500 Unrecouped Balance with Prod. Co.

Before reading any further, take a moment to review paragraph 8 (g) of the exclusive recording artist contract. It states that the "company will retain a reserve against all payable royalties." Some distributors may retain reserves of up to fifty percent (50%) of royalties due new artists in order to be protected from paying royalties on records that could eventually be returned by retailers for credit. In other words, the distributor is concerned that approximately one-half of the records shipped could be returned and therefore royalties won't be payable for these records.

In our sample statement, a twenty-five percent (25%) reserve is imposed. As you can see, in the statement due the production company, $53,450 is automatically deducted from the production company royalties for reserves, while the statement from the production company to the artist shows a deduction of $42,750 for reserves from the royalties due the artist.

Advances are the next amounts deducted from the earned royalties. The distributor deducts (or recoups) the $250,000 advance it paid to the production company while the production company, in its statement to the artist, deducts (recoups) the $50,000 it advanced to the artist.

It is assumed that the distributor/production company contract allows the recoupment of only fifty percent (50%) of video costs of $60,000 and independent promotion costs of $50,000. Therefore, only $30,000 and $25,000 of these respective costs are deducted from the production company and artist royalties.

After deduction of reserves, advances, and various costs, the production company's account has an unrecouped balance of –$122,150 and the artist's account an unrecouped balance of –$115,500. Now you can see why even an artist that achieves a gold record (500,000 units in sales) may earn little, if any, money from record royalties. However, the production company and artist *may* generate more income from additional advances they might obtain for recording a second album. That, of course, will depend on whether the distributor exercises its option with the production company. But, even in today's competitive market, the sales of 200,000 units of a relatively unknown artist's debut album, as is the case here, may be considered a good indicator of the possibility of even greater sales of the artist's follow-up album. So, it is likely that the distributor would exercise its option to have the production company record a second album.

As a result of more restrictive terms of recoupment of costs associated with the production and promotion of recordings, it is becoming increasingly difficult for the production company and the artists to generate significant income from this revenue source. It has, therefore, become increasingly more important for production companies and artists to realize earnings from owning copyrights in the underlying compositions. The next chapter delves deeper into the true "money-maker" in the music industry: the composition copyright.

10

Copyright Principles
The Copyright "Bundle of Rights"

The copyright is the most valuable asset in the music business. That's right! *The most valuable asset.* I want to reiterate that the goals of a successful production company should include the procurement and exploitation of as many copyrights as possible. This needs to be done because, after the delivery of four to six LPs by an artist, the production company's contractual rights to the services of the artist under an exclusive recording agreement will eventually end. In most cases, the record company, rather than the production company, owns the masters and as a result, reaps the benefits of the continued reuse of the masters. While I firmly believe a production company should strive to maintain and fully exploit the many uses of the recordings it owns, the long-term value of the copyright in the composition embodied on the master recording may eventually exceed that of the recording.

Did you ever wonder why Motown Record Company was sold in 1988 for the sum of only $61 million? One reason was that in the years immediately preceding the sale, Motown incurred significant expenses in simply keeping its large business operation afloat. Some industry insiders considered the selling price a paltry sum but it was no paltry sum in my book. You would think that Motown, with over 100 number one hits during its thirty-plus-year span, must have been worth more than that, right? I did as well and decided to take a closer look at what Berry Gordy, Motown's owner, actually sold and doing so clarified the situation for me. Berry Gordy sold the name Motown, the rights to old and future Motown master recordings, and the contractual rights to aging artists whose most recent records hadn't been selling well. What wasn't publicized at the time of the sale was that Berry Gordy maintained his publishing companies, Jobete and Stone Diamond, the entities that hold the ownership interests in thousands of valuable copyrights of the compositions contained on the master recordings that were sold. Many in the industry suspected that the value of those publishing interests exceeded that of the record label he sold. And we were right. Gordy eventually sold his publishing company interests for $320 million. Emerging production/publishing companies should learn the following lessons from this story: (1) get the copyrights; (2) increase the value of the copyrights by promoting the various uses of the songs (remember, Berry Gordy had a hundred number one hits); and (3) hold on to the copyrights.

So, what is this most valuable asset, the copyright? Well, first of all, the copyright isn't just one right, it's actually what many people describe as a "bundle," or a number of exclusive rights. The copyright, or the right to copy, is an intangible property right granted by statute to authors for the protection of their works. The best way to protect an author's work is to register it with the U.S. Copyright Office. Registration can be accomplished by filing a PA (performing arts) registration for published or unpublished musical works or an SR (sound recording) registration for sound recordings. If the same copyright claimant desires to protect the sound recording as well as the underlying musical work, only an SR form needs to be filed. The PA form of registration protects the underlying musical work while the SR form protects the sound recording. Both types of registration give the owner certain statutory including three times the provable damages and payment of the owner's attorney's fees by the party infringing on the work.

These remedies are unavailable to a work that is unregistered. While, in some circumstances, certain unpublished works may be protected by a particular state's common law, authors are urged to pursue protection of their works by registering with the Register of Copyright Office. In order to complete the registration process, the following should be sent to the U.S. Copyright Office: (1) a copy of the work (CD, sheet music or MP-3); (2) a PA (performing arts) or SR (sound recording) form or CO online registration form indicating PA or SR category registration; and (3) the appropriate registration fee.

There are four primary rights of the copyright "bundle of rights" that I am called upon by my clients to protect on a regular basis. These rights are: the **mechanical right**, the **performance right**, the **synchronization right**, and the **derivative right**.

First is the mechanical right. This is the right to mechanically reproduce the musical work. A mechanical reproduction can be a digital download, a vinyl record, a CD, or other such reproduction of the musical work. In order to encourage the ability for one to record and distribute copyrighted works, the copyright law established a compulsory mechanical license. This license establishes a set royalty that must be paid to the copyright owner of the composition for the mechanical reproduction, manufacturing, and distribution of copies of the work. As of the time of this edition, the minimum mechanical royalty rate is 9.1¢ for recordings five minutes or less or 1.75¢ per minute for recordings in excess of five minutes. Therefore, if a production company desires to record a composition written by a writer not affiliated with the production company and without an agreement to the contrary, it or the manufacturer of the vinyl record, CD or digital download (usually the record company) must pay the owner of the copyright of the composition at least the full compulsory mechanical royalty rate of 9.1¢ per mechanical reproduction of the work, in order not to infringe upon the copyright.

Suppose an artist who also happens to be a songwriter exclusively signed to the production company writes all ten (10) of the compositions on his or her album. If the production company's publishing affiliate owns the copyrights of all the compositions, and the full mechanical royalty rate is paid for their use, the publishing company would be entitled to 91¢ in mechanical royalties for each album. If 100,000 albums are distributed, the publishing company would be entitled to $91,000 in mechanical royalties. And just suppose that two of the compositions contained on album are released on two separate digital download singles that are certified gold by the RIAA (representing the sale of at least 500,000 copies) and generate $45,500 each. That's a total of $182,000 in mechanical royalties from the sale of albums and singles.

Sounds like the way to amass a gold mine, huh? Well, I hate to burst your bubble, but most record companies obviously started to believe they were paying copyright owners a "gold mine" worth of royalties. So they began incorporating what has come to be known as *the controlled composition clause* in most artist and production company contracts. The controlled composition clause specifies that any compositions owned or controlled by the artist or production company must be licensed to the record company at three-quarters (3/4) of the statutory compulsory minimum mechanical royalty rate. So, instead of being paid 9.1¢ per copy, the copyright owner is paid three-quarters (3/4) of that amount or roughly 6.8¢ per copy of the composition. In the previous example, if the terms of a controlled composition clause were applied, the total royalties owed to the copyright owner would be reduced to roughly $136,000. The record company's rationale for the controlled composition clause is, by investing in the recording, manufacture, promotion, and distribution of the artist's record, it should be "cut a break" in having to pay the full mechanical royalty rate to the artist. My advice to the artist or production company who has enough clout is to try to get the record company to agree to pay a higher percentage than the three-quarter (3/4) rate or the full statutory minimum mechanical royalty rate.

It is important to note that if the production company decides to manufacture and release recordings on its own, it must pay mechanical royalties to the owners of copyrights of the compositions contained on recordings. Again, the production company owner has to recognize that when he or she reproduces, sells, and gets paid for the recordings all the money they may receive is not for him or her. Not only does the production company have to pay artist and producer royalties, it also has to pay mechanical royalties to the copyright owners of the compositions.

Next is the performance right or the right to publicly perform the composition. This right is usually licensed through the copyright owner's performance right affiliate. Affiliating as a publishing company and songwriter with one of the major performance rights organization's (ASCAP, BMI, or SESAC) is the best way to exploit this right. As I always say, "whenever the music is played somebody gets paid." These organizations are national organizations qualified and staffed to best protect and exploit a composition copyright owner's rights in this area. ASCAP, BMI, and SESAC control a significant number of the copyrights of compositions performed on radio, television stations, in venues, streamed on the Internet or wherever music is performed across the nation. As a result, they have considerable leverage in convincing radio stations, television stations, restaurants, clubs, Internet service providers (Spotify, Rhapsody, etc.) and other users to pay annual fees for the right to use, or publicly perform, any of the songs contained in the respective organization's catalog of affiliated publishers and songwriters. Each of the three organizations aggressively markets it as the best performance rights organization for songwriters and publishers to be affiliated with in order to receive the maximum royalties from the licensing of these rights. ASCAP, BMI, and SESAC each have their own system of tracking and calculating the amount of money each performed composition earns.

Prior to 1990, many experts maintained that BMI was more thorough in canvassing black radio stations and therefore paid larger royalties to owners of copyrights played on these stations. However, over the past two decades ASCAP has proven to be equally competitive in payouts in most genres of music. SESAC, the smallest of the three performance rights organizations, has made significant strides since the beginning of the 21st century, increasing its market share from approximately 5% to 10%. In either case, there is a substantial difference in the amounts of royalties paid for songs that appear on the pop charts as opposed to those on the R&B or country charts. For example, a composition contained on a record that reaches number one on the pop charts may generate 5 to 10 times the earnings of a composition that just tops the R&B or country chart. Another important point to remember is that the royalties earned as a result of licensing the performance rights are based on the number of public performances of the work, not on record sales. If you have a rap mixtape that has sold a half million units with very little, if any, radio play, do not expect a significant royalty check from your performance rights organization. Most of the royalties are paid to copyright owners whose compositions are played on the radio or streamed on the Internet and are therefore "tracked" for purposes to triggering royalty payments. However, for a top charted record that is accumulating millions of streams, selling well and being played on a lot of radio stations, the performance right may challenge the mechanical right as the primary source of income to the composition copyright owner.

Another part of the bundle is the synchronization right. This is the right to synchronize the work from one medium to another and primarily covers situations where a prior copyrighted song is "synchronized" or coupled with a video image, such as a movie, television program, or commercial. When this is done, the user of the prior copyrighted work must first obtain the right to incorporate the song into the video. This right is usually obtained by the means of a license agreement. The terms of such a license may vary. In the case of a song being synchronized into a movie, the movie production company may attempt to "buy out" (pay a one-time flat fee) for the right to use the work for all exploitations of the movie. However, if the copyright owner has leverage, they could attempt to negotiate a separate fee for each type of exploitation of the movie such as its feature film release, DVD or digital release, cable or network and international showings.

In a case where a movie company requests the creation of a composition for both synchronization in the movie, and on the movie's sound track album, the company may demand to co-publish or participate in owning up to 50% of the work. This may be a tough point for the copyright owner to swallow. But, considering a movie company's considerable power to expose and promote a song, such a proposal may be considered a tremendous opportunity.

Last is the derivative right. This is the right to derive a new work from a prior copyrighted work. In 1989, a movie titled *Lean On Me* used a version of the hit composition previously written and made popular by Bill Withers in the seventies. The use of the song as the title of the movie gave rise to the need for the movie's producers to obtain a license from Withers' publishing company. While these are some examples of exploitation of the derivative right, the use of samples of copyrighted works in new works has promulgated the newest and most complex set of issues regarding the derivative right.

Don't sample! (Or be sure to obtain the clearance to use a copyrighted work before you do.)

In an article I wrote for *Agent & Manager* magazine in the early 1990s, I warned: "Rap Managers Beware: Sampling Can Be Hazardous to Your Financial Health." In that article I noted how the use of samples enriched the owners of the sampled copyrights but decreased the earnings of the sampling parties. Well, sampling still occurs today and has financial ramifications for all parties concerned. Better systems have been established to obtain the rights to use the sampled copyrights, but in order to do so, you first have to know what a "sample" is.

The technical definition of sampling is the electronic digital lifting of portions ("samples") of a previously recorded work for insertion in a new master recording. This form of creating derivative works based on prior copyrights came into prominence with the emergence of the rap era that began in the late 1970s. Some of the first popular rap recordings like "Rappers Delight" used the entire rhythm track of the song, "Good Times," previously written by Niles Rodgers and Bernard Edwards, and recorded by members of their group Chic. While the technical definition of sampling requires the lifting and subsequent use of a portion of a prior master recording, the term has also been used to describe the use of a prior copyrighted melody in a new master recording or composition. Although this practice isn't technically considered "sampling," it does raise the same issue of infringing on the copyright of a prior copyrighted composition.

At this point, I think a definition of the term *copyright claimant*, as well as an explanation of the difference between a performing arts (PA) and/or sound recording (SR) form of copyright registration is in order. As I stated previously, under the law of most states, authors of original works may be able to claim common law copyright protection for their work if it can be proved that they are the originator of the work. Filing an eCO form with the U.S. Copyright Office can be the simple and effective method of protecting your work. The eCO form of copyright registration can only be filed online and operates to protect the owner of the composition and/or sound recording from copyright infringement. The eCO form allows you to choose from several different types of copyright registration, including the PA and SR. While the PA type of copyright registration protects the underlying composition, the SR form of copyright registration protects the actual mechanical reproduction of the composition from infringement. The manufacturer of the recording, usually the record company, owns the sound recording copyright, which gives it remedies should infringers copy or duplicate any parts of the recording.

In a true case of sampling, where the master recording of a composition is digitally made a part of a subsequent new recording, the party using the sample must obtain derivative rights from the owners of both the composition and the master recording in order to avoid a potential copyright infringement claim. The new work may be a derivative of the copyright of the composition (owned by the author or publisher and protected by a PA registration) and/or the master recording (owned by the record manufacturer and protected by an SR registration).

It would be best to avoid copyright infringement by obtaining permission from the owner of the work prior to using the work. This is usually achieved by obtaining a license or clearance agreement from the owner in exchange for some form of monetary consideration, e.g., a flat buyout fee for the right to use the works in all mediums or a royalty of some sort.

The smart songwriter or production company owner, capable of creating or attracting creators of powerful product, will build greater value and worth in his or her company by not having to share mechanical, performance, and other royalties with other copyright owners. To further expound on the monetary effect of using samples, you only have to consider the controlled composition clause contained in most production company agreements with record companies, where the record company is already paying the production company three-quarters (3/4) of the minimum statutory mechanical royalty rate or roughly seven cents (7¢) rather than nine cents (9¢) per mechanical reproduction. If your production company achieves a gold record (500,000 units sold), of which just one track contains a melody of a prior copyright-protected composition, the owner of this copyright may demand that you split the copyright to the newly created work with them on a 50-50 basis. Instead of five cents (7¢) per copy, you've just reduced your earnings to three and a half cents (3.5¢) per copy, a substantial difference to your bottom line.

My warning to songwriters or production company owners looking to maximize their company's worth by developing a strong publishing company owning a significant number of copyrights: Don't sample! Don't sample! Don't (and I mean, *Don't*) sample!

If after that, however, you still don't take my advice or just can't help sampling, be sure you obtain a clearance to use the sampled work from one of the sample clearance "houses," as they're called. These small but effective operations will, for a fee, track down the owners of the sampled work and obtain a license agreement for the work's use. Usually these rights are obtained for an advance, which could run into thousands of dollars and may be recouped against an agreed-upon royalty. In some cases, the owner of the infringed-upon work may demand a percentage interest in the ownership of the new work.

Keep the proper perspective in mind. If you hope to build a strong base in the most important asset in the music business, and you, or your company's songwriter-producers are creative enough, I would urge you to maximize your creativity and your assets by not sampling! Remember, maximizing your creativity results in maximizing your assets.

In addition to these top four income-generating rights of copyright, two other rights also prove of the value to copyright owners. **The grand right** allows producers of Broadway plays to adapt non-dramatic versions of compositions for use in the dramatic setting of stage presentations. The plays "Jersey Boys," "American Idiot" and "Motown the Musical" are perfect examples of exploitation of this right. The producers of these shows had to obtain the grand right from the publishers of each song used in these successful plays. Another important right is **the print right**. If anyone prints prepares sheet music of a musical work, they must first obtain the right to do so from the copyright owner. While it's important to remember that these other lesser rights are also part of the copyright "bundle of rights," the mechanical, performance, synchronization, and derivative rights are the key rights that result in generating the bulk of income for songwriters or production companies in today's popular music.

The following exclusive songwriter and co-publishing and administration contracts more fully explain the relationship between the songwriter and co-publishers.

11

Exclusive Songwriter Contract

Analysis of Songwriter/Publishing Company Agreement

CONTRACT	ANALYSIS
Exclusive Songwriter Agreement	**Analysis of Exclusive Songwriter Agreement**
THIS AGREEMENT made and entered into this ____ day of _____, ___, by and between [Name of Production Company's Publishing Company], individually and as Administrator and Co-publisher for [Songwriter/Artist's Name] and/or his publishing designee with offices located at [Address of Production Company's Publishing Company] (hereinafter referred to as "Publishers") and [Songwriter/Artist's Name and Address] (hereinafter referred to as "Writer").	This Agreement, between the production company's publishing company and artist's publishing company (jointly referred to as publishers) and the artist covers his or her exclusive services as a songwriter during the term, which is coterminous with the exclusive recording agreement.

CONTRACT	ANALYSIS
WITNESSETH **WHEREAS,** publisher, [Name of Production Company's Publishing Company] its affiliate [Name of Production Company] and [Name of Production Company's Management Company] have entered into a Co-Publishing, Exclusive Recording (hereinafter "Recording Agreement") and Personal Management Agreement respectively, with Writer or Writer's Publishing Designee of even date and it is hereby the intention of the parties that the term hereof shall be coterminous with the term of the Exclusive Recording Agreement; **NOW, THEREFORE,** for good and valuable consideration the receipt of which is hereby acknowledged by each party hereto, it is agreed as follows:	
1. EMPLOYMENT. Publisher hereby employs Writer to render Writer's services as a songwriter and composer and otherwise as may hereinafter be set forth. Writer hereby accepts such employment and agrees to render such services exclusively for Publisher during the term hereof, upon the terms and conditions set forth herein.	1. Under this agreement, the artist/songwriter is purposely deemed an employee of the publishers which gives the publisher the benefit of a prolonged period of ownership of the copyrights written during the term. This concept is more fully explained in the analysis of paragraph 6 of this Agreement.
2. TERM. The initial term of this agreement shall commence upon the date hereof and continue for the initial term of the Recording Agreement. It is the intention of the parties hereto that the term hereof	

CONTRACT

shall be coterminous with the term of the Recording Agreement (a copy of the pertinent part thereof is hereby attached hereto and incorporated herein and marked as attachment "A"), as same may be renewed or extended from time to time. Accordingly, each extension or renewal of the term of the Recording Agreement shall automatically extend or renew the term hereof for the same period. The phrase "the term hereof" or "the term of this agreement" as used in this agreement, shall refer to the initial and any extension or renewal terms hereof in accordance with the foregoing. Notwithstanding anything to the contrary contained herein, in the event either the Management, Co-Publishing or Songwriters Agreements are terminated for any reason prior to the end of that term of the Recording Agreement, all of the agreements between the parties shall be terminated at that time.

3. GRANT OF RIGHTS. Writer hereby irrevocably and absolutely assigns, conveys and grants to Publisher, its successors and assigns (a) all rights and interests of every kind, nature and description in and to all original musical compositions and all original arrangements of musical compositions in the public domain which have heretofore been written, composed or created by Writer, in whole or in part, alone or in collaboration with others, including but not limited to the titles, lyrics

ANALYSIS

3. During the term of the Agreement, the artist grants and assigns all rights and interests, in the copyrights written, to the publishers including the right to:

CONTRACT

and music thereof and all worldwide copyrights and renewals and extensions thereof under the present or future laws throughout the world, to the extent any of the foregoing shall not heretofore have been conveyed by Writer to an unrelated third party; and (b) all rights and interests of every kind, nature and description in and to the results and proceeds of Writer's services hereunder, including but not limited to the titles, lyrics and music of all original musical compositions and of all original arrangements of musical compositions in the public domain and all universe-wide copyrights and renewals and extensions thereof under any present or future laws throughout the world, which shall be written, composed or created by Writer during the term hereof, in whole or in part, alone or in collaboration with others; and (c) all rights and interests of every kind, nature and description in and to all original musical compositions and all original arrangements of musical compositions in the public domain which are now directly or indirectly owned or controlled by Writer, in whole or in part, along or with others, or the direct or indirect ownership or control of which shall be acquired, by Writer during the term hereof, in whole or in part, alone or with others, as the employer or transferee of the writers or composers thereof or otherwise, including the titles, lyrics and music thereof and all universe-wide copyrights and renewals and extensions

ANALYSIS

CONTRACT

thereof under any present or future laws throughout the universe; all of which musical compositions, arrangements, rights and interests Writer hereby warrants and represents are and shall at all times be Publisher's exclusive property as the sole owner thereof, free from any adverse claims or rights therein by any other party (all such musical compositions and arrangements hereinafter being referred to as "Compositions").

Without limiting the generality of the foregoing, Writer acknowledges that the rights and interests hereinabove set forth include Writer's irrevocable grant to Publisher, its successors and assigns, of the sole and exclusive right, license, privilege and authority throughout the entire universe with respect to all Compositions, whether now in existence or whether created during the term hereof, as follows:

(a) To exploit and license others to perform through sound recordings the Compositions publicly or privately, for profit or otherwise, by means of public or private performance, radio broadcast, television, or any and all other means of media, whether now known or hereafter conceived or developed.

(b) To substitute a new title or titles for the Compositions or any of them and to make any arrangement, adaptation, translation, dramatization or transposition of any or all

ANALYSIS

(a) exploit and license the compositions in all media and by any means;

(b) substitute or change the title, lyrics or music contained in the composition;

CONTRACT

of the Compositions or of the titles, lyrics or music thereof, in whole or in part, and in connection with any other musical, literary or dramatic material, and to add new lyrics to the music of any Compositions or new music to the lyrics of any Composition, all as Publisher may deem necessary or desirable in its best business judgment.

(c) To secure copyright registration and protection of the Compositions in Publisher's or it's designee's name or otherwise, as Publisher may desire, at Publisher's own cost and expense, and at Publisher's election, including any and all renewals and extensions of copyright under any present or future laws throughout the universe, and to have and to hold said copyrights, renewals and extensions and all rights existing thereunder, for and during the full term of all said copyrights and all renewals and extensions and all rights existing thereunder, for and during the full term of all said copyrights and all renewals and extensions thereof.

(d) To make or cause to be made, and to license others to make master records, transcriptions, soundtracks, processing and any other mechanical, electrical or other reproductions of the compositions, in whole or in part, in such form or manner and as frequently as Publisher shall determine, including the right to synchronize the Compositions with sound motion pictures and to use,

ANALYSIS

(c) secure copyright registration in the publisher's name;

(d) license for mechanical, synchronized use, etc.;

CONTRACT

manufacture, advertise, license or sell such reproductions for any and all purposes, including without limitation private and public performances, radio broadcast, television, and motion picture, wired radio, phonograph records and any and all other means or devices, whether now known or hereafter conceived or developed.

(e) To print, publish and sell, and to license others to print, publish and sell, sheet music, orchestrations, arrangements and other editions of the Compositions in all forms, including, without limitation, the inclusion of any or all of the Compositions in song folios, compilations, song books, mixed folios, personality folios and lyric magazines with or without music.

(f) Any and all other rights now or hereafter existing in all Compositions under and by virtue of any common law rights and all copyrights and renewals and extensions thereof including so-called small performance rights. Writer grants to Publisher, without any compensation other than as specified herein, the perpetual right to use and publish and to permit others to use and publish Writer's name (including any professional name heretofore or hereafter adopted by Writer), Writer's photograph or other likeness, or any reproduction or simulation thereof, and biographical material concerning Writer, and the titles of any and all of the

ANALYSIS

(e) print or otherwise publish the song's music and/or lyrics;

(f) use the artist's name and likeness for purposes of the exploitation of the works;

The artist/songwriter also warrants and represents that he or she has the full right and power to fulfill the terms of the contract, and in no way will the performance of the contract infringe on the rights of others. This provision is very important to the publishers because it requires the songwriter to guarantee that he or she has not entered into an agreement with another party, such as a competing publisher, which would interfere with his or her performance of this contract.

This grant of rights provision is very broad and should be a cause of concern for the songwriter. On behalf

CONTRACT

Compositions, in connection with the printing, sale, advertising, performance, distribution and other exploitation of the Compositions, and for any other purpose related to the business of Publisher, its affiliated and related companies, or to refrain therefrom. This right shall be exclusive during the term hereof and nonexclusive thereafter. Writer shall not authorize or permit the use of Writer's name or likeness, or any reproduction or simulation thereof, or biographical material concerning Writer, for or in connection with any musical compositions, other than by or for Publisher. Writer grants Publisher the right to refer to Writer as Publisher's "Exclusive Songwriter and Composer" or to use any other similar and appropriate appellation, during the term hereof.

4. EXCLUSIVITY. During the term of this agreement, Writer shall not write or compose, or furnish or convey, any musical compositions, titles, lyrics, or music, or any rights or interests therein, nor participate in any manner with regard to same, for or to any party other than Publisher, nor permit the use of his name or likeness as the writer or co-writer of any musical composition by any party other than Publisher.

5. WARRANTIES, REPRESENTATIONS, COVENANTS AND AGREEMENTS. Writer hereby warrants, represents, covenants and agrees as follows: Writer has

ANALYSIS

of the songwriter, I would demand certain limits be placed on the publisher's rights to change or alter the compositions, exploit the compositions by any means, and the use of the artist's name.

A recognizable and memorable example of why the songwriter should want to limit the publisher's right to change or alter the lyrics of a composition occurred during the 1996 presidential campaign. At some of the campaign stops of presidential candidate Bob Dole, the lyrics of the hook of the hit song, "Soul Man," were sung, "I'm a Dole Man." Isaac Hayes, one of the writers of the original song, objected to the use of the tune in this manner. But under the terms of this agreement, a songwriter would forfeit their right to object to the publisher's approval of such an alteration of the lyrics.

In situations where I have represented songwriters, I have been able to negotiate limits on this type of provision by requiring the publishers to first obtain the consent of the songwriter for potentially objectionable uses such as this.

CONTRACT

the full right, power and authority to enter into and perform this Agreement and to grant to and vest in Publisher all rights herein set forth, free and clear of any and all claims, rights and obligations whatsoever; all of the Compositions and all other results and proceeds of the services of Writer hereunder, including all of the titles, lyrics and music of the Compositions and each and every part thereof, delivered and to be delivered by Writer hereunder are and shall be new and original and capable of copyright protection throughout the entire world; no Composition shall, either in whole or in part, be an imitation or copy of, or infringe upon, any other material, or violate or infringe upon any common law or statutory rights of any party including, without limitation, contractual rights, copyrights and rights of privacy; and Writer has not sold, assigned, leased, licensed or in any other way disposed of or encumbered any Composition, in whole or in part, or any rights herein granted to Publisher, nor shall Writer sell, assign, lease, license or in any other way dispose of or encumber any of the Compositions, in whole or in part, or any of said rights, except under the terms and conditions hereof.

6. POWER OF ATTORNEY. Writer hereby irrevocably constitutes, authorizes, empowers and appoints Publisher or any of its officers Writer's true and lawful

ANALYSIS

6. A Power of Attorney is granted from the artist to the publishers allowing the publishers to execute, sign or take such other action necessary to assign the rights granted therein to the

CONTRACT

attorney (with full power of substitution and delegation), in Writer's name, and in Writer's place and stead, or in Publisher's name, to take and do such action, and to make, sign, execute, acknowledge and deliver any and all instruments or documents, which Publisher from time to time may deem desirable or necessary to vest in Publisher, its successors and assigns, all of the rights or interests granted by Writer hereunder, including without limitation, such documents as Publisher, its successors and assigns, the worldwide copyrights for all compositions for the entire term of copyright and for any and all renewals and extensions under any present or future laws throughout the universe. Notwithstanding the foregoing, Writer acknowledges that he (or she) is Publisher's employee for hire, and that Publisher is accordingly the author of all Compositions for all purposes of the 1909 or 1976 Copyright Law or any succeeding Copyright Law.

7. COMPENSATION/ROYALTIES. Provided that Writer shall duly perform the terms, covenants and conditions of this agreement, Publisher shall pay Writer, for the services to be rendered by Writer hereunder and for the rights acquired and to be acquired by Publisher hereunder, the following compensation/royalties collected from a source on the Compositions:

ANALYSIS

publishers. The artist/songwriter also acknowledges that he or she is the publisher's employee for hire for copyright law purposes.

Under copyright law, the copyright vests with the "author" of a work who is usually the writer. However, if the writer is writing as an employee and within the scope of his employment with the publisher, the publisher, not the writer, is deemed the "author". The very important aspect of this designation pertains to the length of time the ownership of a work may be retained by the publisher. For example, if the publisher is the employer of a writer for hire, it will retain the ownership of the work for the shorter of 120 years from the date of creation of the work or 95 years from the date of publication of the work. If the writer is not designated an employee for hire, he or she is the author and the copyright in the work will vest in the author's name and will exist for the life of the author, plus 70 years. Moreover, if the writer is not working as an employee for hire for the publisher, the writer may grant the work to the publisher by way of a transfer or assignment and will have the right to terminate the transfer to the publisher between the 35th and 40th year after the execution of the grant or the date of first publication of the work. The right to terminate requires written notice to the publisher. However, because the designation of the writer as an employee may result in the publisher having to bear the responsibilities of extending the benefits of employment (a salary, equipment, workers' compensation insurance,

CONTRACT

(a) Ten cents ($.10) per copy for each copy of sheet music in standard piano/vocal notation and each dance orchestration printed, published and sold in the United States and Canada by Publisher or its licensees, for which payment shall have been received by Publisher, after deduction of returns.

(b) Ten percent (10%) of the wholesale selling price of each printed copy of each other arrangement and edition printed, published and sold in the United States and Canada by Publisher or its licensees, for which payment shall have been received by Publisher, after deduction of returns, except that in the event that any Compositions shall be used or caused to be used, in whole or in part, in conjunction with one or more other musical compositions in a folio, compilation, song book or other publication, Writer shall be entitled to receive that proportion of the foregoing royalty which the number of Compositions contained therein shall bear to the total number of musical compositions therein.

(c) Fifty percent (50%) of any and all net sums actually received (less any costs for collection) by

ANALYSIS

unemployment insurance, etc.) most publishers are actually opting for the writer's assignment of the copyright rather than seeking the long term rights they could obtain by having the writer considered their employee.

(a) You might ask, "How is the songwriter compensated?" Well, this paragraph states that the songwriter will receive 10 cents per each copy of sheet music. The range for this royalty may vary from contract to contract from 5 cents to 12 cents or, in some rare cases, 50% of the publisher's receipts, which equals approximately 30 cents.

(c) The songwriter is paid 50% of the net receipts collected by the publisher for the licensing of mechanical,

CONTRACT	ANALYSIS
Publisher in the United States from the exploitation in the United States and Canada by licensees of mechanical rights, grant rights, electrical transcription and reproduction rights, motion picture and television synchronization rights, dramatization rights and all other rights therein (except print rights, which are covered in (a) and (b) above, and public performance rights, which are covered in (d) below), whether or not such licensees are affiliated with, owned in whole or in part by, or controlled by Publisher.	synchronization and other use rights (except public performance).
(d) Writer shall receive his public performance royalties throughout the world directly from the performing rights society with which he is affiliated, and shall have no claim whatsoever against Publisher for any royalties received by Publisher from any performing rights society which makes payment directly (or indirectly other than through Publisher) to Writer, authors and composers. If, however, Publisher shall collect both the Writer's and Publisher's share of performance income directly and such income shall not be collected by Writer's public performance society, Publisher shall pay to Writer's fifty percent (50%) of all such net sums which are received by Publisher in the United States from the exploitation of such rights in the Compositions, throughout the world.	(d) The songwriter's portion of public performance royalties (50% of the amount allocated for the composition) is usually not collected by the publisher. It is instead paid from the performance rights organization (BMI, ASCAP, SESAC) directly to the writer. The publisher's portion is also paid direct to the publishers by the performance rights organizations and, in the case of a co-publishing arrangement, pursuant to an "Across the Board Deal", the songwriter's publishing company ("Participant") would be entitled to 50% of the publisher's share of 50% (or 25% of the whole), if the songwriter was the sole writer.

CONTRACT	ANALYSIS

CONTRACT

(e) Fifty percent (50%) of any and all net sums, after deduction of foreign taxes, actually received (less any costs of collection) by Publisher in the United States from the exploitation of the Compositions in countries outside of the United States and Canada (other than public performance royalties, which are covered in (d) above), whether from collection agents, licensees, sub-publishers or others, and whether or not same are affiliated with, owned in whole or in part by, or controlled by Publisher.

(f) Publisher shall not be required to pay any royalties on professional or complimentary printed sheet music copies which are distributed gratuitously to performing artists, orchestra leaders and disc jockeys or for advertising, promotional or exploitation purposes. Furthermore, no royalties shall be payable to Writer on consigned copies unless paid for, and not until such time as an accounting therefore can properly be made.

(g) Royalties as hereinabove specified shall be payable solely to Writer in instances where Writer is the sole author of a Composition, including the lyrics and music thereof. However, in the event that one or more other songwriters are authors together with Writer of any Composition (including songwriters employed by Publisher to add, change or translate the lyrics or to revise or change the music),

CONTRACT

the foregoing royalties shall be divided equally among Writer and the other songwriters unless another division of royalties shall be agreed upon in writing between the parties concerned and timely written notice of such division is submitted to Publisher prior to payment.

(h) Except as herein expressly provided, no other royalties or monies shall be paid to Writer.

(i) Writer agrees and acknowledges that Publisher shall have the right to withhold from the royalties payable to Writer hereunder such amount, if any, as may be required under the provisions of all applicable Federal, State and other tax laws and regulations, and Writer agrees to execute such forms and other documents as may be required in connection therewith.

(j) In no event shall Writer be entitled to share in any advance payments, guarantee payments or minimum royalty payments which Publisher shall receive in connection with any subpublishing agreement, collection agreement, licensing agreement or other agreement covering the Compositions or any of them.

8. ACCOUNTING. Publisher shall compute the royalties earned by Writer pursuant to this agreement between Writer and Publisher or its affiliates, whether now

ANALYSIS

8. The Writer is accounted to on a semi-annual basis before March 31 and September 30 of each year for the sixth month period ending December 31st and June 30th. It's important to

CONTRACT

in existence or entered into at any time subsequent hereto, on or before March 31st for the semiannual period ending the preceding December 31st and on or before September 30th for the semiannual period ending the preceding June 30th, and shall thereupon submit to Writer the royalty statement for each such period together with the net amount of royalties, if any, which shall be payable after deducting any and all unrecouped advances and chargeable costs under this agreement or any other agreement. Each statement submitted by Publisher to Writer shall be binding upon Writer and not subject to any objection by Writer for any reason unless specific written objection, stating the basis thereof, is sent by Writer to Publisher within one (1) year after the date said statement is submitted. Writer or a certified public accountant on Writer's behalf may, at Writer's expense, at reasonable intervals (but not more frequent than once each year), examine Publisher's books insofar as same concern Writer, during Publisher's usual business hours and upon reasonable notice, for the purpose of verifying the accuracy of any statement submitted to Writer hereunder. Publisher's books relating to activities during any accounting period may only be examined as aforesaid during the two (2) year period following service by Publisher of the statement for said accounting period.

ANALYSIS

note that, in this Agreement, all unrecouped advances and costs under any and all other agreements may be recouped (cross collateralized) from royalties earned under this contract. Any objection by the writer to the accounting statements rendered must be made in writing before the end of one year after the receipt of the statement. A representative who has been appointed by the writer may examine the records of the publisher within two years after receipt of each statement.

CONTRACT	ANALYSIS
9. COLLABORATION. Whenever Writer shall collaborate with any other person in the creation of a Composition, the Composition shall be subject to the terms and conditions of this agreement, and Writer warrants, represents and agrees that prior to such collaboration Writer shall advise such other person of this exclusive agreement and shall further advise such other person that all Compositions so created must be published and owned by Publisher. In the event of any such collaboration, Writer shall notify Publisher of the nature and extent of such other person's contribution to the Composition, and Writer shall cause such other person to execute a separate songwriter's agreement with Publisher covering the Composition, which agreement shall set forth the division of the songwriter's royalties between Writer and such other person, and Publisher shall make payment accordingly.	9. Suppose the writer collaborates with another writer in the composition of a song. Under the terms of this paragraph, the writer must inform such co-writer of the existence of this agreement and that the entire composition, including his or her contribution, shall be published by the publisher by way of a separate songwriters contract between the collaborator and publisher. While this provision can cause concern for a collaborator who is already signed with another publisher for the publishing of his or her works, it is an effective tool which enables the publisher to obtain valuable copyright interests from new, unaffiliated writers who collaborate with the publisher's more experienced writers.
10. SEPARATE AGREEMENTS. If Publisher so desires, Publisher may request Writer to execute a separate standard songwriters contract in Publisher's customary form with respect to each Composition hereunder. Upon such request, Writer shall promptly execute and deliver such separate agreement, and upon Writer's failure to do so, Publisher shall have the right, pursuant to the terms and conditions hereof, to execute such separate agreement on behalf of Writer.	10. In order to further document the Writer's share of each composition, the publisher may (and should) require the writer to execute a single song or separate songwriter's contract. This document is a valuable supplement to the Exclusive Songwriter Contract because it can: 1) serve as a separate document transferring the writer's copyrights of compositions to the publishers on a song by song basis; and 2) establish, in a writing executed by the parties, the agreement of multiple songwriters (if that is the case) as

CONTRACT

Such separate agreement shall supplement and not supersede this agreement. In the event of any conflict between the provisions of such separate agreement and this agreement, the provisions of this agreement shall govern. The failure of either of the parties hereto to execute such separate agreement, whether such execution is requested by Publisher or not, shall not affect the rights of each of the parties hereunder, including but not limited to the rights of Publisher to all of the Compositions written, composed or acquired by Writer during the term hereof.

11. WRITER'S SERVICES. (a) Writer shall perform his required services hereunder conscientiously, and solely and exclusively for and as requested by Publisher. Writer is a writer for hire hereunder, and all Compositions are acknowledged by Writer to be works made for hire. Writer shall duly comply with all requirements and requests made by Publisher in connection with its business as set forth herein. Writer shall deliver manuscript copy or tape copy of each Composition immediately upon the completion or acquisition of such Composition. Publisher shall use its reasonable efforts in its best business judgment to exploit any or all of said Compositions hereunder, but Publisher's failure to exploit said compositions shall not be deemed a breach hereof. Publisher at its sole discretion shall reasonably make studio facilities

ANALYSIS

to their percentage of the songwriter's share of each composition. This provision goes further to grant the publisher the right to execute such an agreement on the writer's behalf should the writer fail to do so after being requested.

11. Do you remember my explanation of the reason for wanting the writer to compose on a work for hire basis for the publisher? From the historical perspective prior to the mid-70s, most songwriters had to sign exclusive songwriters agreements with publishers that didn't allow them to participate in copyright ownership at all. The songwriting duo, Ashford and Simpson, is an example of that. During their heyday of writing such hits as "You're All I Need to Get By," "Ain't Nothing Like the Real Thing," and "Ain't No Mountain High Enough," they were employed as exclusive songwriters for the Motown affiliate, Jobete. Although Ashford and Simpson gave up any publishing interest in these songs (and any other compositions they created during the term of their agreement with Motown) they did obtain added benefits as a result of the magnificent ongoing

CONTRACT	ANALYSIS

CONTRACT

available for Writer so that Writer, subject to the supervision and control of Publisher, may produce demonstration records of the Compositions, and Writer shall have the right to perform at such recording sessions. Publisher shall also have the right to produce demonstration records hereunder. Writer shall not incur any liability for which Publisher shall be responsible in connection with any demonstration record session without having obtained Publisher's prior written approval as to the nature, extent and limit of such liability. In no event shall Writer incur any expense whatsoever on behalf of Publisher without having received prior written authorization from Publisher. Writer shall not be entitled to any compensation (except for such compensation as is otherwise provided for herein) with respect to services rendered in connection with any such demonstration recording sessions. Publisher shall advance the costs for the production of demonstration records, subject to the foregoing, and one-half (1/2) of such costs shall be deemed additional advances to Writer hereunder and shall be recouped by Publisher from royalties payable to Writer by Publisher under this agreement or any other agreement between Writer and Publisher or its affiliates. All recordings and reproductions made at demonstration record sessions hereunder shall become the sole and exclusive property of Publisher, free of any claims

ANALYSIS

marketing and cross-promotion of the recordings of these great songs that Motown provided. However, in the middle of the 1990s it was reported that this hit songwriting duo were able to "get paid" as much as $25 million by issuing bonds, secured against payment of future songwriters royalties for these songs. Well, in this paragraph, under the heading Writer's Services, certain circumstances are detailed to, in essence, help further document the existence of the employer/employee relationship between the publisher and the writer. There are certain phrases that are intended to highlight the employer/publisher's control over the writer, such as:

- Writer shall perform as requested by publisher;
- Writer shall comply with all requirements and requests of publisher;
- Writer shall promptly deliver tape copies of compositions to publisher;
- Writer shall perform on and record demos pursuant to and under the direction and control of publisher (without compensation, I might add!);
- Writer shall bear half of the costs of the demos; said costs being recoupable from royalties;
- Writer shall appear for photographic and other sessions or promotional engagements (once again, without further compensation) at the request and direction of the publisher;

CONTRACT

whatsoever by Writer or any person deriving any rights from Writer.

(b) Writer shall, from time to time, at Publisher's reasonable request, and whenever same will not unreasonably interfere with prior professional engagements of Writer, appear for photography, artwork and other similar purposes under the direction of Publisher or its duly authorized agent, appear for interviews and other promotional purposes, and confer and consult with Publisher regarding Writer's services hereunder. Writer shall also cooperate with Publisher in promoting, publicizing and exploiting the Compositions and for any other purpose related to the business of Publisher. Writer shall not be entitled to any compensation (other than applicable union scale if appropriate) for rendering such services, but shall be entitled to reasonable transportation and living expenses if such expenses must be incurred in order to render such services.

12. **UNIQUE SERVICES.** Writer acknowledges that the services to be rendered by Writer hereunder are of a special unique, unusual, extraordinary and intellectual character which gives them a peculiar value, the loss of which cannot be reasonably or adequately compensated in damages in an action at law, and that a breach by Writer of any of the provisions of this agreement will cause Publisher great and irreparable injury and damage. Writer

ANALYSIS

All these requirements and acknowledgments on behalf of the writer, further support the publisher's contention that the compositions were composed by the writer on an employee for hire basis. This may entitle the publisher to retain the rights for the time prescribed under the copyright law regarding works created on a work for hire basis.

As mentioned earlier, most current publishers don't actually exert this type of control over their songwriter's activities and therefore opt for the songwriter to assign the copyright to them instead of being considered their employee for hire.

CONTRACT

expressly agrees that Publisher shall be entitled to the remedies of injunction and other equitable relief to enforce this agreement or to prevent a breach of this agreement or any provision hereof, which relief shall be in addition to any other remedies, for damages or otherwise, which may be available to Publisher.

13. ACTIONS. Publisher shall have the exclusive right to take such action as it deems necessary, either in Writer's name or its own name or in both names, against any party to protect all rights and interests acquired by Publisher hereunder. Writer, shall cooperate fully with Publisher in any controversy which may arise or litigation which may be brought concerning Publisher's rights and interests acquired hereunder. Publisher shall have the right, in its discretion, to employ attorneys and to institute or defend against any claim, action or proceeding, whether for infringement of copyright or otherwise, and to take any other necessary steps to protect the right, title and interest of Publisher in and to each Composition and, in connection therewith, to settle, compromise or in any other manner dispose of any such claim, action or proceeding and to satisfy or collect on any judgment which may be rendered. If Publisher shall recover on a judgment or as a result of a settlement with respect to any claim, action or proceeding for copyright infringement

ANALYSIS

CONTRACT

initiated by Publisher, all of Publisher's expenses in connection therewith, including, without limitation, attorney's fees and other costs, shall first be deducted, and fifty percent (50%) of the net proceeds shall be credited to Writer's account.

14. INDEMNITY. Writer hereby indemnifies, saves and holds Publisher, its successors and assigns, harmless from any and all liability, claims, demands, loss and damage (including counsel fees and court costs) arising out of or connected with any claim or action by a third party which is inconsistent with any of the warranties, representations or agreements by Writer in this agreement, and Writer shall reimburse Publisher, on demand, for any loss, cost, expense or damage to which said indemnity applies. Publisher shall give Writer prompt written notice of any claim or action covered by said indemnity, and Writer shall have the right, at Writer's expenses, to participate in the defense of any such claim or action with counsel of Writer's choice. Pending the disposition of any such claim or action, Publisher shall have the right to withhold payment of such portion of any monies which may be payable by Publisher to Writer under this agreement or under any other agreement between Writer and Publisher or its affiliates as shall be reasonably related to the amount of the claim and estimated

ANALYSIS

14. In this "indemnity" clause, the writer covers any losses sustained by the publisher for any breach of warranty by the writer. It is similar to the ones contained in the other agreements contained in this book. If the publishers receive a claim, the writer may participate in his/her defense at their own cost after receiving notice of the claim from the publisher. Pending the disposition of such a claim, the publishers may withhold any royalties due the writer in an amount reasonably related to the amount of the claim and the estimated legal fees it will take to proceed with the case.

CONTRACT

counsel fees and costs. If Publisher shall settle or compromise any such claim or action, the foregoing indemnity shall cover only that portion (if any) of the settlement or compromise which shall have been approved in writing by Writer, and Writer hereby agrees not unreasonably to withhold any such approval. Notwithstanding the foregoing, if Writer shall withhold approval of any settlement or compromise which Publisher is willing to make upon advice of counsel and in its best business judgment, Writer shall thereupon deliver to Publisher an indemnity or surety bond, in a form satisfactory to Publisher, which shall cover the amount of the claim and estimated counsel fees and costs, and if Writer shall fail to deliver such bond within ten (10) business days, Writer shall be deemed to have approved of said settlement or compromise.

15. NOTICES. Any written notices which Publisher shall desire to give to Writer hereunder, and all statements, royalties and other payments which shall be due to Writer hereunder, shall be addressed to Writer at the address set forth at the beginning of this agreement until Writer shall give Publisher written notice of a new address. All notices which Writer shall desire to give to Publisher hereunder shall be addressed to Publisher at the address set forth at the beginning of this agreement until Publisher shall give Writer written notice of a new

ANALYSIS

CONTRACT

address, and a courtesy copy of all such notices shall also be given to [Publisher Attorney's Name and Address]. All such notices shall either be served by hand (to an officer of Publisher if Publisher shall be the addressee) or by registered or certified mail, postage prepaid, or by telegraph, charges prepaid, addressed as aforesaid. The date of making personal service or of mailing or of depositing in a telegraph office, whichever shall be first, shall be deemed the date of service.

16. ENTIRE AGREEMENT. This agreement supersedes any and all prior negotiations, understandings and agreements between the parties hereto with respect to the subject matter hereof. Each of the parties acknowledges and agrees that neither party has made any representations or promises in connection with this agreement or the subject matter hereof not contained herein.

17. MODIFICATION, WAIVER, INVALIDITY, AND CONTROLLING LAW. This agreement may not be cancelled, altered, modified, amended or waived, in whole or in part, in any way, except by an instrument in writing signed by the party sought to be bound. The waiver by either party of any breach of this agreement in any one or more instances shall in no way be construed as a waiver of any subsequent breach of this agreement (whether or not of a similar

ANALYSIS

CONTRACT

nature). If any part of this agreement shall be held to be void, invalid or unenforceable, it shall not affect the validity of the balance of this agreement. This agreement shall be deemed to have been made in the State of New York and its validity, construction and effect shall be governed by the laws of the State of New York applicable to agreements wholly performed therein. This agreement shall not be binding upon Publisher until signed by Writer and countersigned by a duly authorized officer of Publisher.

18. ASSIGNMENT. Publisher shall have the right to assign this agreement or any of its rights hereunder to any party which is or shall be a subsidiary, affiliate or parent or to any party which shall acquire all or a substantial portion of Publisher's stock or assets.

19. DEFINITIONS. For the purposes of this agreement, "party" means and refers to any individual, corporation, partnership, association or any other organized group of persons or the legal successors or representatives of the foregoing. Whenever the expression "the term of this agreement" or words of similar connotation are used herein, they shall be deemed to mean and refer to the initial term of this agreement and any and all renewals, extensions, substitutions or replacements of this agreement, whether expressly indicated or otherwise.

ANALYSIS

18. The publisher has the unlimited right to assign this contract to any party that may purchase all (or a substantial portion) of the ownership of the publisher. This provision favors the writer by requiring the purchasing party to obtain, at least, a substantial portion of the publisher's business. This may give some assurance to the writer that the purchasing party is at least comparable in size to the publisher and has the wherewithal to succeed in its obligations to exploit the writer's copyrights.

CONTRACT

20. SUSPENSION AND TERMINATION. If Writer shall fail, refuse or be unable to submit to Publisher two songs a month or shall otherwise fail, refuse or be unable to perform his material obligations hereunder, Publisher shall have the right, in addition to all of its other rights and remedies of law or in equity, to suspend the term of this agreement and its obligations hereunder by written notice to Writer, or, in the event such failure, refusal or inability shall continue for longer than six (6) months, to terminate this agreement by written notice to Writer. Any such suspension shall continue for the duration of any such failure, refusal or inability, and, unless Publisher notifies Writer to the contrary in writing, the then current term hereof shall be automatically extended by the number of days which shall equal the total number of days of suspension. During any such suspension Writer shall not render services as a songwriter and/or composer to any other party or assign, license or convey any musical composition to any other party.

21. HEADING. The heading of clauses or other divisions hereof are inserted only for the purposes of convenient reference. Such headings shall not be deemed to govern, limit, modify or in any other manner affect the scope, meaning or intent of the provisions of this agreement or any part thereof, nor

ANALYSIS

CONTRACT

shall they otherwise be given any legal effect.

22. CO-OWNERSHIP AND ADMINISTRATION. Notwithstanding any provision to the contrary herein contained, all Compositions shall be equally owned by Publisher and by Writer's designee, and shall be exclusively administered by Publisher, all in accordance with the terms and provisions of the Co-publishing Agreement annexed hereto as Exhibit "A".

ADDITIONAL CLAUSES

23. OTHER ARRANGEMENTS. Writer has entered or is entering into a recording contract with Publisher's production/record company affiliate. Notwithstanding any provision to the contrary herein contained, it is the intent of the parties hereto that the term of this agreement be coterminous with the term of said recording contract or of any successor or replacement agreement. Accordingly in the event said record company affiliate or its assignee fails to exercise any renewal option with respect to the recording contract or the successor or replacement agreement, Publisher shall not have the right to exercise any renewal option hereunder; further, any extension, renewal, suspension or termination of the recording contract or of the successor or replacement agreement by said record company

ANALYSIS

22. This paragraph further acknowledges that, pursuant to the co-publishing and administration agreement between the parties, the artist/songwriter's publishing company shall own an interest in the compositions.

23. This clause notes that the publisher/writer arrangement is part of an Across the Board Deal, and as such, the Recording and Exclusive Songwriters Agreements are coterminous.

CONTRACT

affiliated or its assignee shall automatically and without further notice extend, renew, suspend or terminate this agreement in like manner.

24. RECOUPMENT. It is understood and acknowledged that any and all charges or advances against royalties under this agreement which are not recouped by Publisher may be recouped by Publisher's record company affiliate or its assignee from any and all royalties earned by Writer under the aforementioned recording contract or its successor or replacement agreement, and that any and all charges or advances against royalties under said recording contract or its successor or replacement agreement which are not recouped by said record company or its assignee may be recouped by Publisher from any and all royalties earned by Writer hereunder.

25. INDUCEMENT. Writer acknowledges that this agreement with Publisher is further consideration for Publisher's record company affiliate to enter into the recording contract hereinabove referred to, and that Writer is entering into this agreement to induce said record company affiliate to enter into said recording contract.

 IN WITNESS WHEREOF, the parties hereto have executed this agreement as of the day and year first above written.

ANALYSIS

CONTRACT

WRITER   PUBLISHER

By: _____

[Name of Publisher]
individually and as
Administrator for [Songwriter/
Artist Name] Publishing
Designee

ANALYSIS

12

Co-Publishing and Administration Contract

Breakdown of Co-Publisher/Publisher Agreement

CONTRACT	ANALYSIS
Co-Publishing and Administration Agreement	**Analysis of Co-Publishing and Administration Agreement**

THIS AGREEMENT made this ____ day of _____, by and between [Name of Production Co.'s Publishing Company] with offices located at [address of Publishing Company], (hereinafter referred to as "Company") and [Name and address of Songwriter/Artist] and/or his publishing designee (hereinafter referred to as "Participants").

WITNESSETH

WHEREAS, it is the intention of Company and Participants that they shall jointly own Participant's

The across the board deal arrangement for signing artists and songwriters became popular during the mid-1970s. Near the end of that decade, courts determined that the multiple contracts that provide the basis of this type of relationship could be voided unless the production company would allow the artist/songwriter to retain at least a 50% interest in the ownership of their copyrights. This Co-Publishing agreement, is a reflection of the effect of that rule.

It is an agreement between the production company's publishing company (referred to "Company")

CONTRACT

portion of the musical compositions (hereinafter referred to as "Composition" and collectively referred to as "Compositions") acquired by Company pursuant to Company's Exclusive Songwriter's Agreement of even date herewith with [Songwriter/Artist name] (hereinafter Songwriter's Agreement"), so that the entire universe-wide right, title and interest including the copyright, the right of copyright and any and all renewal rights, in and to Participants portion of the Compositions shall be owned by Company and by Participants in the percentages described below:

PERCENTAGES:
Company—50%
Participants—50%

WHEREAS, the Compositions shall be registered for copyright in the names of Company and Participants in the Copyright Office of the United States of America.

WHEREAS, Company and/or its affiliates [Production & Management Companies Names], have entered into a Management Agreement and Exclusive Recording and Songwriter's Agreement with [Songwriter/Artist name] (hereinafter Recording Agreement) of even date and it is hereby the intention of the parties that this agreement, the Management, Songwriter's and Recording Agreements be coterminous.

ANALYSIS

and the songwriter's publishing company (referred to as "Participant").

The contract's preamble describes and states that the Company and Participant shall share in the ownership of the copyrights owned hereunder on a 50%/50% basis.

CONTRACT

NOW THEREFORE, for good and valuable consideration the receipt of which is hereby acknowledged by each party hereto, it is agreed as follows:

1. Company and Participants shall jointly own Participant's portion of the Compositions conveyed pursuant to the Exclusive Songwriter's Agreement between Company and [name of Songwriter/ Artist] dated _____, in the shares described above so that all the worldwide right, title and interest, including the copyrights, the right to copyright and any renewal rights therein and thereto shall be owned 50%— Company and 50% Participant. The phrase, "Participant's portion of the composition(s)," as used herein, shall be equivalent to Participant's pro rata percentage of songwriters contribution to the compositions.

2. The Compositions shall be registered for copyright by Company in the names of Company and Participants in the office of the Register of Copyrights of the United States of America. If any Composition has heretofore been registered for copyright in the name of Participants, Participants shall simultaneously herewith deliver to Company an assignment of the appropriate interest therein, in form acceptable to Company.

ANALYSIS

1. The "Participant's portion" of the composition relates only to the percentage of the copyright owned by the songwriter/artist should the songwriter/artist collaborate with another writer. If the songwriter/artist writes only 50% of the song, the Participant's portion of ownership of the composition shall only be 50% which, according to this contract, will be equally shared by the Participant and the Company.

2. The Company will be joint owner of the Participant's portion of the copyright. All the compositions acquired pursuant to the related exclusive songwriter's agreement shall be registered with the U.S. Copyright Office in the name of the Company and Participant.

CONTRACT	ANALYSIS
3. Participants hereby assign, transfer and grant to Company, its successors and assigns, licensees and subpublishers, the rights and responsibilities set forth below in and to the Compositions:	3. The Participant agrees to grant to the Company a number of important rights, such as:
(a) The exclusive right to manage and administer throughout the Licensed Territory, all rights of every kind, nature and description in and to the Compositions, together with the right to manage and administer all copyrights and renewals or extensions thereof.	(a) the right to manage and administer Participant's interest in the copyrights throughout the territory;
(b) Participants hereby appoint Company as its sole exclusive agent throughout the Licensed Territory, for the purpose of collecting all income from sales and uses of the Compositions. Participants grant to Company the right to collect, on Participants' behalf, all gross income received heretofore unpaid, and now payable and all income which becomes payable during the term of this Agreement, from the date of original copyrights to the Compositions to be the effective date hereof and from all sales and uses of the Compositions, subject to accountings hereunder.	(b) the right to collect income from the exploitation of the compositions;
(c) The exclusive right to issue all licenses with respect to mechanical and electrical reproduction of the Compositions throughout the Licensed Territory on phonograph records, compact discs, prerecorded tapes, piano rolls and transcriptions, or by any	(c) the exclusive right to execute and issue all licenses with respect to mechanical reproduction of the compositions;

CONTRACT	ANALYSIS
other method now known and hereafter devised for sound reproduction and the licensing of the Compositions for such purposes throughout the Licensed Territory upon terms within the sole discretion of Company.	
(d) The exclusive right to exploit and have others to perform through sound recordings of compositions for profit or otherwise by means of public performance, radio broadcast or any other means of media now known or hereafter conceived or developed throughout the universe.	(d) the right to exploit performances of the compositions by means of radio, television, Internet or other media;
(e) The exclusive right to grant licenses for the recording of the Compositions in and with motion pictures and television productions produced throughout the Licensed Territory, or making copies of the recordings thereof, and importing such copies into all countries of the world.	(e) the right to license the compositions for synchronization with motion pictures, television and other productions;
(f) The exclusive right to print, publish and sell printed music throughout the Licensed Territory in the form of sheet music, arrangements, song books, albums, portfolios or educational works and to authorize others to exercise said right. In connection with the foregoing and without any compensation other than as specified herein, Participants grant to Company the non-exclusive right to use and publish and to permit others to use and publish the names of any and all	(f) the right to license and publish the compositions in printed music form;

CONTRACT	ANALYSIS
authors and/or writers of the Compositions, (including any other professional name heretofore or hereafter adopted by such authors and/or writers), likenesses of, voice and sound effects and biographical material, or any reproduction or simulation thereof and titles of the Compositions. Company shall not use any artwork, photographs, likenesses of or biographical material relating to said individuals unless same have been approved by Participants or submitted to Company by Participants.	
(g) The right to substitute a new title or titles for the Compositions and to make any change, arrangement, parody, adaptation, translation, or dramatization of the Composition, in whole or in part, and in connection with any other musical, literary or dramatic material as Company may deem expedient or desirable.	(g) the right to substitute new titles or change or adapt the lyrics of the compositions; While the Company is granted broad powers under this agreement, the attorney for the Participant may attempt to negotiate certain limits on the company's discretion to administer the compositions. It's possible that some forms of exploitation of the compositions may not appeal to the Participant, such as the use of a composition in a political commercial or objectionable movie or television program. The Participant may also object to the revision of a composition's lyrics. Under the terms of this agreement, the Participant is granting the Company the sole right and discretion to make these decisions, which could come back to haunt the Participant/Songwriter/Artist.
4. The term of this agreement shall commence upon the date hereof and shall continue for the	4. As a result of this contract being part of an "Across The Board Deal", it is coterminous with the

CONTRACT	ANALYSIS
term of the Recording Agreement, (a copy of the pertinent part thereof are hereby attached hereto and incorporated herein and marked as attachment "A"), as same may be renewed or extended from time to time. Accordingly, each extension or renewal of the term of the Recording Agreement shall automatically extend or renew the term hereof for the same period. The phrase "the term hereof" or "the term of this agreement" as used in this agreement, shall refer to the initial and any extension or renewal terms hereof in accordance with the foregoing. Notwithstanding anything to the contrary herein, in the event either the Management, Co-Publishing or Songwriters Agreement are terminated for any reason prior to the end of that term of the recording agreement, all of the agreements between the parties shall terminate at that time.	Management, Exclusive Songwriters and Recording Agreements, which means that if one of these agreements end, they are all terminated.
5. Company shall pay directly to Participants his publisher share and to the composition's writers their shares of the net income share due Participants and the composition's writers actually received and derived by company from the Compositions. "Net Income", as used herein, shall mean the gross receipts derived by Company from the Compositions less the following: (a) Collection or other fees customarily and actually charged by any collection agent;	5. The Participant shall receive its fifty percent (50%) publisher's share after all writers first receive their shares of net income. As you know in business in general the net income is defined as gross receipts less expenses. In the Publishing business that would include collection fees, administration charges charged by a third party, actual out of pocket administration or exploitation expenses such as mailings, copies, demo recordings, lead sheet transcribing, and attorneys fees directly related to a defense of claims

CONTRACT

(b) Administration Fees charged by any Third Party Administrator;

(c) Actual, out-of-pocket administrative and exploitation expenses of Company with respect to the Composition for registration fee, advertising and promotion expenses directly related to the Compositions, the costs of transcribing for lead sheets, and the costs of producing demonstration records;

(d) Attorneys' fees directly related to the defense of claims respecting the Compositions, if any, actually paid by Company;

6. The performing rights in the Compositions in the percentage as listed above, to the extent permitted by law, shall be assigned to and licensed by BMI or ASCAP as the case may be, which shall be and hereby is authorized to collect and receive all monies earned from the public performance of the Compositions and to pay directly to Company and Participants their share of one-hundred percent (100%) of the amount allocated by said performance rights society as the publisher's share of public performance fees.

7. All mechanical royalties for the Compositions shall be collectible by such collection agent as may be designated by Company, provided however, that Company, may issue the mechanical licenses directly to said record company and collect mechanical royalties directly

ANALYSIS

regarding the interests granted hereunder.

6. The performance rights organizations (ASCAP, BMI and SESAC) that license performing rights are authorized under this contract to pay royalties due the parties directly to the Company and Participant. In other words, the company does not have to account to the Participant for the share of the performance rights royalties because they are paid directly to each party.

7. All mechanical royalties are collected directly by the Company, which accounts to and pays the Participant according to the accounting provision paragraph 8 hereunder which requires semi-annual statements within 90 days of the semi-annual periods ending June 30 and December 31 of each year.

CONTRACT	ANALYSIS
therefrom in which case there shall be no collection fee as referred to Paragraph 5 hereinabove. 8. (a) Company shall render to Participants statements showing the amount of royalties payable hereunder for the semi-annual periods ending June 30th and December 31st, respectively, accompanied by payment of any royalties shown to be due in such statements within 90 days of the end of said semi-annual periods. (b) At any time within one (1) year after any royalty statement is rendered to Participants hereunder, Participants shall have the right to give Company written notice of its intention to examine Company's books and records with respect to such statement. Such examination shall be commenced within six (6) months after the date of such notice, at Participants' sole cost and expense, by any certified public accountant or attorney designated by Participants, provided he is not then engaged in an outstanding examination of Company's books and records on behalf of a person other than Participants. Such examination shall be made during Company's usual business hours at the place where Company maintains the books and records which relate to Participants and which are necessary to verify the accuracy of the statement or statements specified in Participants' notice to Company and	8. This provision not only deals with the requirements for accounting to the Participant, but also indicates the Participant's right to audit or review the company's accounting. The Participant's right to audit is outlined in this paragraph and is limited to a prescribed period of one (1) year after receipt of the accounting statement. In my opinion, this provision is arguably too detail oriented, indicating who may audit (CPA/and/or Attorney not involved in current audit of books), when the audit may occur, (during regular hours, only once a year) and why, (to determine accuracy) which, if not challenged by an action by Participant within two (2) years, shall be deemed final and conclusive. This provision is pretty restrictive and as attorney for the Participant I would try to negotiate a less restrictive audit provision giving the Participant greater flexibility in auditing the Company's books. In addition, for agreements subject to California law, a 2004 statute extends the period of time the participant may object and/or file suit to three (3) years regardless of language to the contrary in the contract.

CONTRACT	ANALYSIS
Participants' right to inspect Company's books and records shall be only as set forth in this subparagraph and Company shall have no obligation to produce such books and records more than once with respect to each statement rendered to Participants. Unless notice shall have been given to Company as provided in this subparagraph, each royalty statement rendered to Participants shall be final, conclusive and binding upon Participants and shall constitute an account stated. Participants shall be foreclosed from maintaining any action, claim or proceeding against Company in any forum or tribunal with respect to any statement or accounting rendered hereunder unless a court of competent jurisdiction within two (2) years after the due date of such statement or accounting. (c) Participants acknowledge that Company's books and records contain confidential trade information. Neither Participants nor its representatives will communicate with others or use on behalf of any other person any facts or information obtained as a result of such examination of Company's books and records. 9. Each party hereto shall give the other the equal benefits of any warranties or representations which it obtains or shall obtain under any agreements affecting the Compositions.	

CONTRACT

10. Upon written request by Company, Participants shall promptly deliver to Company (a) typed lyric sheets of the Compositions and (b) copies of photographs, likenesses, and biographical material of the writer or writers of the Compositions.

11. Company shall have the sole right to prosecute, defend, settle and compromise all suits, claims and actions respecting the Compositions, and generally to do and perform all things necessary concerning the same and the copyrights therein, to prevent and restrain the infringement of copyrights or other rights with respect to the Compositions. In the event of the recovery of Company of any monies, less an amount equal to the expense of obtaining said monies, including counsel fees shall be deemed additional gross receipts hereunder. Company will credit Participants' account hereunder with Participants' applicable share of such monies as set forth in Paragraph 5 hereof, and will pay Participants, within thirty (30) days after receipt of such monies by Company, the net credit balance of Participants' account, if any Company will not settle any claim respecting the Compositions without Participants' consent, which consent shall not be unreasonably withheld.

12. The rights of the parties hereto in and to the Compositions shall

ANALYSIS

11. The Company shall also have the sole right to proceed in any action with respect to the Composition (e.g., claim for copyright infringement by a party who samples a composition subject to this agreement) and, if successful, will split the proceeds equally with Participant, less any expenses.

12. A publishing administration contract differs from a co-publishing

CONTRACT

extend for the term of the copyright of the Compositions and of any derivative copyrights therein in the United States of America throughout the rest of the world and for the terms of any renewals or extensions thereof in the United States of America and throughout the rest of the world.

13. Participants hereby warrant and represent that they are under no disability, restriction, or prohibition with respect to their right to enter into this agreement and to grant to Company all of the rights granted herein, and that the exercise by Company of any and all of the rights granted to Company in this agreement will not violate or infringe upon any common law or statutory rights of any person, firm or corporation, including, without limitation, contractual rights, copyrights and rights of privacy. The rights granted herein are free and clear of any claims, demands, liens or encumbrances. Participants agree to and do hereby indemnify, save and hold Company, it assigns, licensees, and its and their directors, officers, shareholders, agents and employees harmless from any and all liabilities, claims, demands, loss and damage (including attorneys' fees, and court costs) arising out of or connected with any claim by a third party which is inconsistent with any of the warranties, representations, covenants, or agreements made by Participants herein

ANALYSIS

agreement in an important aspect. The parties' rights to the composition (most importantly, the right of the company to administer and own 50% of Participant's portion of the Copyright) extend for the full term of the copyright and any renewals or extensions. If this deal were solely a publishing administration contract the company would not have any ownership in the copyrights of the Participants, but would only have the exclusive right to administer the copyrights for a fixed period of time usually for a set percentage (10%–25%) of the income generated during the term after which the rights of administration would revert back to the Participant. Therefore, in a publishing administration contract the Participant receives the dual benefit of retaining the right of ownership of the copyrights, while affiliating with a publisher, who, for a fee, uses its expertise to more fully exploit the participant's catalog of copyrights.

CONTRACT

and Participants agree to reimburse Company, on demand, for any payment made by Company at any time after the date hereof with respect to any liability or claim to which the foregoing indemnity applies. Pending the determination of any such claim, Company may withhold payment of royalties or other monies hereunder, provided that all amounts so withheld are reasonably related to the amount of said claim and the estimated attorney's fees in connection therewith, and provided further that Participants shall have the right to post a bond in an amount reasonably satisfactory to Company by a bonding Company reasonably satisfactory to Company, in which event Company shall not withhold payments as aforesaid.

14. In the event that Participants receive a bona fide offer from a third party (the "Third Party Offer") to purchase all or any portion of Participants interest in a composition or of any of them and Participants desire to sell such interest, Participants agree to first offer in writing to sell such interest to Company (the "First Offer") upon all the terms and conditions set forth in the Third Party Offer. Such First Offer shall specify all of the terms and conditions of the Third Party Offer and in the event Company does not, within thirty (30) days after receipt by Company of the First Offer, accept the First Offer, then Participants shall

ANALYSIS

14. This provision, a right of first refusal clause, allows the company to match any third party offer made to the Participant for its ownership share of a particular copyright or the entire catalog. This is accomplished by imposing certain time limitations and restrictions on the company's right to match a third party offer which, as a result, provides the company the opportunity to maintain an ownership interest in copyrights it may have created value in through its exploitation efforts. Of course the Participant's attorney may ask that a similar provision be inserted in favor of the Participant should the company desire to sell its interests.

CONTRACT	ANALYSIS
have the right to accept the Third Party Offer; provided, however, that the sale to such third party shall be consummated within one hundred twenty (120) days after receipt of the First Offer by Company and, provided further, that the sale to such third party shall be upon all of the terms and conditions contained in the First Offer. If such sale is not consummated, Participants shall not sell all or any portion of its interest in the Composition or any of them without first offering to sell such interest to Company as hereinbefore set forth. 15. Any notice, consent, approval, demand, or other communication to be given or sent to the other party hereunder must be in writing and shall be deemed to have been duly given or sent if delivered personally or if sent by registered mail to the address first hereinabove stated or to such other address as either party may send to the other party by like notice. Except as otherwise herein stated, the date of mailing or of actual personal delivery of any such communication shall be deemed the date upon which such communication was given or sent. 16. This Agreement shall not be deemed to give any right or remedy to third party whatsoever unless said right or remedy is specifically granted to such third party by the terms hereof.	

CONTRACT

17. The parties hereto shall execute any further documents including, without limitation, assignments of copyrights, and do all acts necessary to fully effectuate the terms and provisions of this agreement. Participants hereby irrevocably appoint Company or any of its officers as its true and lawful attorney-in-fact to make, sign, execute, acknowledge, and deliver in its name any and all instruments which Company may deem desirable to vest in Company, its successors, assigns, and licenses any or all of the rights herein granted to Company.

18. Company may enter into sub-publishing agreements with, or assign, or license any of its rights hereunder to, one or more other persons, firms, or corporations for any one or more countries of the world. In the event Company enters into a subpublishing or administration agreement for any country of the world with a company affiliated with or otherwise related to Company, such agreement shall be deemed to have been made with an independent third party. Participants acknowledge that Company has the right to administer and publish compositions other than the Compositions.

19. Company shall have the right to assign, sell or license this Agreement in whole or in part at any time during the term hereof to any person, firm or corporation, including

ANALYSIS

17. The Participant appoints the Company as its attorney-in-fact, enabling the company to execute licenses, copyright forms, transfers, and assignments in the Participant's name should the Participant not be available to authorize such actions. This assures the Company that it may vest the rights granted hereunder if the Participant inadvertently fails to do so.

18. The Company also has the right to enter into sub-publishing contracts with other companies. In this agreement, it is also specified that the Company may enter into a contract with an affiliate for this purpose. If so the affiliate will be deemed an independent third party to the Company. This may allow the Company to, in essence, double dip, by allowing its foreign affiliate to take a fee off the top before the Company is required to split the balance with Participant. The Participant's attorney may desire to have this fee lowered or eliminated entirely to prevent the double dipping aspects of such a transaction.

19. You'll see here that the company also has the right, without restrictions, to assign this contract. The Participant could consider this unrestricted right a potential problem and

CONTRACT

but not limited to any of Company's affiliates or subsidiaries. However, no such assignment, sale or license shall relieve Company of its obligations hereunder without the express written consent of participants.

20. This Agreement sets forth the entire understanding between the parties, and cannot be changed, modified, or cancelled except by an instrument signed by the party sought to be bound.

21. It is understood and acknowledged that any and all charges or advances against royalties made by Company to Participant under this and/or any other agreement between the parties which are not recouped by Company may be recouped by Company's production company affiliate or its assignee from any and all royalties earned by Participant under the aforementioned recording agreement or its successor or replacement agreement and that any and all charges or advances against royalties under said recording agreement or its successor or replacement agreement which are not recouped by said production company or its assignee may be recouped by Company from any and all royalties earned by Participant hereunder.

This Agreement shall be governed by and construed under the laws of the State of New York

ANALYSIS

may seek to have it limited. You see, in many instances, a Participant may execute this type of contract because of a special relationship with specific personnel of the Company and therefore will not want the Company to assign the agreement to another Company without its prior consent.

21. This last paragraph allows the cross-collateralization of publishing royalties against all advances from the Company or any of its affiliates. The company may insist on its inclusion because of the sizable up front investment its production company affiliate has made in recording the songwriter/artist. As I indicated earlier, since significant costs of videos and independent promotion are routinely made recoupable from record royalties, the only effective stream of earnings for the songwriter/artist may be the copyright earnings subject to this agreement. I strongly recommend resisting any attempt to have this important stream of earnings used to offset the costs of any other agreement executed by the artist/songwriter.

CONTRACT	ANALYSIS
applicable to agreements wholly performed therein. IN WITNESS WHEREOF, the parties have executed this Agreement the day and year above set forth. "PARTICIPANT" _____ "COMPANY" _____	

13

Statement and Analysis of Copyright Earnings
How the Copyright Money Flows

The following statement and analysis of composition copyright earnings will help you see the flow of monies to the songwriter and his or her co-publishing affiliate under the terms of a Co-publishing agreement.

As I indicated earlier, the copyright is the most important asset in the music business, particularly to the artist-songwriter, because if his or her recording agreement is properly negotiated, the songwriter's earnings should not be cross-collateralized with the recording agreement and used to help recoup the myriad costs associated with the recording process. Therefore, while an artist-songwriter may not realize artist royalties for his or her recording services due to the high costs associated with producing and marketing the records, that same artist-songwriter may realize income from composition copyright earnings from the first sale or airplay of his or her records. In today's music business, this may make the difference in the artist surviving from one record project to the next.

The following statement of copyright earnings is for a fictitious composition titled "Can't Get Enough" and it tracks the earnings generated from the exploitation of the performance, mechanical, derivative, and synchronization rights of the song. Keep in mind that the earnings presented here are for only one composition. Suppose the artist-songwriter had written eight to ten other songs contained on the album which "Can't Get Enough" appeared on. If so, you could multiply the album earnings by eight to ten times and, I guarantee you, you'll see why the copyright is so valuable. And remember, if "Can't Get Enough" is sampled on another record ten years from now or recorded by another artist during that time, the money just keeps rolling in.

I once read an article about William Devaughn, the artist-songwriter who wrote one hit in the 1970s, titled "Be Thankful for What You've Got." That song had the memorable hook: "Diamond in the back, sun roof top, diggin' the scene with a gangster lean . . ." He says that while it was his only hit, with the multiple uses, continued air play, and the sampling of the song since it was released, he's earned over $1 million from that composition alone over the years. As I always say, whenever the music is played, somebody gets paid!

In the typical co-publishing arrangement the Production Company's publishing unit (publisher) administers (handles the business of) the artist/songwriter's songs and is granted a 50% interest in the copyrights. The artist/songwriter retains the other 50% in the name of their own publishing company (co-publisher.) In exchange for 25% of the earnings derived from the copyrighted works the publisher agrees to use its best efforts to protect, exploit, collect income, and account for such income to the co-publisher and songwriter (In some cases, the publisher may receive an additional 10 to 15% as an administration fee.)

This following statement and analysis cover the four primary income-generating rights of the copyright's "bundle of rights" and their resulting income stream. The first income stream is from the exploitation of the performance right.

---

1) PERFORMANCE RIGHT

Publisher, co-publisher and songwriter all affiliate with either ASCAP, BMI, or SESAC to license copyrights for performance. If ASCAP, BMI, or SESAC determines that the composition earned a total of $10,000 in royalties and pays 50% each directly to the publisher(s) (in this case 25% to the publisher and 25% to the co-publisher) and 50% directly to the songwriter.

Earnings:

$10,000 as determined by performance rights organization's royalty calculation

ASCAP/BMI/SESAC

Pays $10,000.00 Royalties Directly to:

Publisher (25%)	Co-publisher (25%)	Songwriter (50%)
$2,500	$2,500	$5,000

As I explained in the section on copyright principles, this right is usually exploited by one of the Big Three performance rights organizations, BMI, ASCAP, or SESAC, pursuant to an affiliation agreement between the performance rights organization, the publisher, and the songwriter. Under the terms of these agreements, the monies earned from the song by the performance rights organization are divided 50% to publishers and 50% to songwriters and paid directly to them from the performance rights organization. In this example, that amount is $10,000, with the publisher and co-publisher being paid $2,500 each and the songwriter $5,000. Keep in mind that if there are multiple publishers (as in this case) or songwriters for a particular composition, these payments must be pro-rated according to each party's interest in the composition.

The second stream of income from the copyright is derived from the exploitation of the mechanical right.

---

2) MECHANICAL RIGHT

Publisher issues mechanical license to Record Company requiring payment of a mechanical royalty of 9.1¢ Minimum Statutory Rate (M.S.R) or 6.8¢ (3/4s of M.S.R.) per mechanical reproduction.

Earnings:

200,000	CD albums
100,000	Digital albums
100,000	Digital Singles
400,000	Total Units containing mechanical reproductions of the composition entitled: "Can't Get Enough"
× 9.1¢	Mechanical royalty per unit
$36,400	Total mechanical royalties owed to publisher by record company

Record Company—Pays
Total Mechanical
Royalties of $36,400 directly to publisher

Publisher—Keeps 25%
Total Mechanical Royalties ($9,100)
Pays 75% ($27,300) to

Co-publisher and Songwriter
Pursuant to Co-publishing Agreement

The mechanical right is exploited through the use of a mechanical license issued by the copyright owner (usually the publisher of the composition) to the record company who manufactures and distributes the recording. Usually, as a result of the application of the controlled composition clause of the exclusive recording artist agreement, the record company pays only three-quarters (3/4) of the minimum statutory mechanical royalty rate of 9.1¢ or 6.8¢ per mechanical reproduction of the composition. However, in this example, we will assume that the record company pays the full minimum statutory mechanical royalty rate of 9.1¢ per mechanical reproduction. "Can't Get Enough" sold a total of 400,000 units containing the copyrighted work, so a total of $36,400 is payable from the record company to the publisher. You may recall that under the terms of the Co-publishing contract, the publisher is allowed to collect the entire amount of mechanical royalties due from the record company. The publisher, in turn, is also required to pay the co-publishing company and songwriter, on a semiannual basis, 75% of the mechanical royalties collected. In my example, the publisher is entitled to collect $36,400 from the record company and must pay 75% of the monies ($27,300) when it submits its account to the co-publisher and songwriter. It's important to note that as the publisher only has to account to the co-publisher and songwriter on a six-month basis, it is allowed to earn extra income by holding the songwriter's royalties until the six-month payout. This is because the U.S. Copyright Act requires manufacturers and distributors to pay mechanical royalties to the copyright owners on a quarterly basis. Consequently, the publisher, who collects the mechanical royalties from the record company every three months, is allowed to earn interest on the money it owes the songwriter until it is required to pay the songwriter after six months.

The derivative right is the third income-generating source.

Suppose a movie company makes a movie titled *Can't Get Enough*, the theme and story of which are substantially similar to the lyrics of the composition. In order not to infringe on the copyright of the composition, the movie company must license the right to base the story on the lyrics of the composition for a one-time payment ($25,000, for example) to the publisher. Under the

3) DERIVATIVE RIGHT

Movie Company makes movie based on lyrics of the copyrighted composition

Earnings:
Flat Buyout of $25,000

Movie Company—Pays
Entire $25,000 to Publisher

Publisher—Keeps
25% ($6,250)

Pays 75% ($18,750) to

Co-publisher and Songwriter
Pursuant to Co-publishing Agreement

---

terms of the Co-publishing contract, the publisher would pay 75% of the fee, in this case $18,750, to the co-publishing company and songwriter.

The synchronization right is the last source of income we'll consider in this example.

As covered in the copyright principles section, the synchronization right is the right to synchronize the copyright from one medium to another (audio to video). In my example, the master recording of "Can't Get Enough" is incorporated in a made-for-television movie. The network pays a one-time flat buyout fee of $10,000 for this right. This amount is also paid directly to the publisher, who accounts for 75% (or $7,500) to the co-publisher and songwriter pursuant to the Co-publishing agreement.

With respect to the derivative right and synchronization right, keep in mind that, while in our example, a one-time flat buyout fee of all uses of the product (digital downloads, DVD, cable, overseas sales, etc.) was paid for these rights, it is possible to have it negotiated so that separate payments will be made for the

4) SYNCHRONIZATION RIGHT

Television movie uses master recording of "Can't Get Enough".

Earnings:
Flat buyout fee of $10,000:

Movie Company—Pays
Entire $10,000 to Publisher

Publisher—Keeps
25% ($2,500)

Pays 75% ($7,500) to

Co-publisher and Songwriter
Pursuant to Co-publishing Agreement

---

various uses of the product. In other words, it is possible for the copyright owner to be paid one fee for the movie to run in theaters, and additional amounts for DVDs, foreign runs, and other ancillary uses of the movie.

Summary of Copyright Earnings of Copyright titled "Can't Get Enough"

	Total Earned	Publisher's Share	Co-publisher/ Songwriter's Share
1) Performance Income	$10,000.00	$2,500.00	$7,500.00
2) Mechanical Income	$36,400.00	$9,100.00	$27,300.00
3) Derivative Income	$25,000.00	$6,250.00	$18,750.00
4) Synchronization Income	$10,000.00	$2,500.00	$7,500.00
TOTAL	$81,400.00	$20,350.00	$61,050.00

Looking at the bottom-line figures of this example should also help you realize the importance of the publisher's share of copyright income. That is why many artists and songwriters attempt to publish their own works, thereby keeping the publisher's share for themselves instead of co-publishing with a larger publishing company and splitting the publisher's share equally.

14

Personal Management Contract
A Preview

Never to be discounted, the personal management contract and the statement and analysis of management earnings deal with the very important manager/artist relationship. Its place in this book has nothing to do with its level of importance. A manager's role in the development and guidance of an artist's career is crucial. A manager's job is to help the artist navigate his or her career through the uncharted, shark-ridden waters that the music business emulates at times. In these times, it seems a manager must be as multidimensional and multimedia savvy as possible. The ability for artists to cross over from the music business into television, movies, merchandising, endorsement, sponsorship and other ventures is greater now than ever before. Just consider artists like Carrie Underwood, Drake, Lady Gaga, etc. These artists, like their predecessors such as P Diddy, Dr. Dre and the late Whitney Houston, all started in music, but expanded the breadth of exploitation of their brands to include not only television and movies but also consumer product development (Ciroc/Revolt-PDiddy, Beats by Dre-Dr. Dre) as well. Managers have the responsibility of recommending the proper time, venue, and mediums to expose and exploit the many talents of artists—a big responsibility, particularly when you consider the manager holds the fate of the artist's career in his or her hands.

While managing an artist's musical activities may be the genesis of the artist's career, a manager's outlook should be focused on building and maintaining a long, successful career for the artist. My dad always told me to "look with the long view," in other words, think about what you'll be doing twenty- to thirty-years from now.

A perfect example of managing with a "long view" is displayed by the recent success of the Tamar Braxton, the youngest of five sisters who all have been singing together for over 20 years. Her eldest sister, Toni Braxton became a superstar solo performer in the 1990s and for years Tamar was relegated to being a backup singer. After an unsuccessful attempt at a solo career early in the new millennium, Tamar continued her role backing her sister, until her husband and manager, Vincent Herbert, fresh off of his success as the producer for Lady Gaga, took control of his wife's career and started making big moves. The 2010 launch of the WeTV series, "Braxton Family Values" not only struck a chord with the reality show market, but also chronicled the rise of Tamar's new solo career effort as well as her sister Toni's comeback to superstardom. For the Braxtons, Herbert, and his management partner Troy Carter, the television show was a stroke of genius that not only exposed Toni to her old fans but developed new ones, not just for her, but for the burgeoning solo career of Tamar, who went on to score two, number one charting singles and an album in *Billboard* magazine. Just think—twenty years. Now *that's* the long view.

> "... a manager's outlook should be focused on building and maintaining a long, successful career for the artist."

As you review the terms of, and comments to, the sample personal management agreement and statement and analysis of the manager's earnings, bear in mind that due to the "across the board" aspect of the manager's relationship with the artist, the manager cannot earn a commission on recording or copyright earnings generated by the artist. After all, the manager is already profiting from these areas pursuant to their recording and co-publishing agreements with the artist. The manager's commissions will only apply to exploitation of the artist's other talents or income-generating opportunities resulting from the success of such talents. However, with the recent explosion of ancillary earning opportunities available to successful musical artists, the manager's, as well as the artist's potential for earning big bucks from the their career is greater than ever before.

CONTRACT

PERSONAL MANAGEMENT AGREEMENT

AGREEMENT made as of the day of _____, by and between [Name and Address of Production Company's Management Company] (hereinafter sometimes referred to as "Manager") and [Individual Group Members Names and Addresses], jointly and individually and collectively professionally known as "[Group Name]" (hereinafter sometimes individually and collectively referred to as "Artist").

WHEREAS, Artist is desirous of engaging the services of Manager to act as Artist's personal advisor and counselor and to attend to certain business details in connection with Artist's professional career in the entertainment industry; and

WHEREAS, Manager is willing to become associated with Artist and act as the manager for Artist upon the terms and conditions hereinafter set forth;

ANALYSIS

ANALYSIS OF PERSONAL MANAGEMENT AGREEMENT

This contract, as with most contracts in the music business, binds all the members of a group, both individually and collectively. If the contract terminates for one group member, it will still be binding for the other group members. When Justin Timberlake first signed a recording agreement as a member of the group, N'Sync, each member of the group was signed individually as well as collectively. When he decided to quit the group and go solo, the record company exercised its right to record him as a solo artist. Although the company had the right to continue to record the remaining members of N'Sync, the company has not done so.

As stated in the preamble of this contract, the role of a manager is to provide the services of a personal advisor and counselor to the artist, attending to certain business details in connection with the artist's career. In many instances, artists look to managers to finance or bankroll their career

CONTRACT

WHEREAS, Manager, its record company and publishing company affiliates have entered into an Exclusive Recording, Co-Publishing and Songwriters Agreement, respectively, with Artist or Artist designees of even date and it is hereby the intention of the parties that the term hereof shall be coterminous with the term of the Exclusive Recording Agreement.

NOW, THEREFORE, in consideration of the foregoing and the mutual promises and covenants hereinafter contained, it is agreed as follows:

1. Artist hereby engages Manager as Artist's sole and exclusive personal manager in the entertainment industry throughout the world during the Term of this Agreement, and Manager hereby accepts such engagement subject to the terms and conditions set forth herein. The term of this Agreement shall commence as of the date hereof and shall continue for the term of the Recording Agreement (a copy of the pertinent part thereof are hereby attached hereto and incorporated herein and marked as "Attachment A"), as same may be renewed or extended from time to time. Accordingly, each extension or renewal of the term of the Recording Agreement shall automatically extend or renew the term hereof for the same period. The phrase "the term hereof" or "term of this agreement" as used in this

ANALYSIS

endeavors. While this may be the case in some instances (as you will see in certain provisions of this contract), the manager is not a "bank" and is under no obligation to finance any of the artist's activities or pay personal bills for the artist while the artist is pursuing his or her career.

1. When the artist engages a manager it is usually done on an exclusive basis. In other words, the artist has only one manager during the term of the contract. As will be discussed later in paragraph 5 of this agreement while the management relationship is exclusive to the artist, it is not exclusive to the manager, which means the manager is free to represent other artists during the term of the contract.

CONTRACT

agreement, shall refer to the initial and any extension of renewal of terms hereof in accord with the foregoing. Notwithstanding anything to the contrary herein, in the event the Management, Co-Publishing or Songwriter's Agreements are terminated for any reason prior to the end of that term of the recording agreement, all of the agreements between the parties shall terminate at that time.

2. Manager agrees, subject to Artist's availability and cooperation, to perform the following personal management services, at the request of Artist, in connection with Artist's activities in the entertainment industry:

(a) advise and counsel in the selection of any literary, artistic and musical material;

(b) advise and counsel in any and all matters pertaining to any public relations and advertising for Artist;

(c) advise and counsel with relation to the adoption of the proper format for presentation of Artist's talents and in the determination of proper style, mood and setting therefor;

(d) advise, counsel and direct in the selection of any artistic talent to work with Artist;

(e) advise and counsel with regard to general practices in the

ANALYSIS

2. Under the terms of this contract, the manager agrees to provide, at the request of the artist, advice and counsel in various areas. This includes the selection of material, matters relating to public relations, format and presentation of the artist's performance, and selection of artistic talent to work with the artist. The manager also advises as to general practices of the entertainment industry with respect to compensation and terms of contracts in the industry. In regard to the manager offering counsel to the artist in respect of compensation and terms of contracts it is important for the artist to insist upon the manager obtaining advice from a competent attorney as to these matters. As I indicated earlier, compensation and terms of contracts in this industry change so rapidly as a result of such dynamics as developing technology and business conditions (i.e., mergers, takeovers and bankruptcies) it is incumbent on managers to reach out to the attorney, whose job it is to keep abreast of these changes in order to best serve the interests of the artist. Please note that in paragraph

CONTRACT

entertainment and amusement industries, and with respect to compensation and terms of contracts in such industries;

(f) advise and counsel concerning the selection of theatrical agencies and persons, firms and corporations to procure employment and engagements for Artist;

(g) negotiate any and all agreement(s) pertaining to Artist's services, but only to the extent permitted by law (Artist agreeing in any event to obtain Manager's prior written approval of each of same); and

(h) use Manager's reasonable efforts to endeavor to advance promising aspects of Artist's career.

3. Artist agrees that Manager is not expected to, nor shall Manager procure or secure employment for Artist. Manager is not to perform

ANALYSIS

2(h) of the contract the manager is required to "use manager's reasonable efforts to endeavor to advance promising aspects of the artist's career." This is a great provision to have in the contract if you're the manager. The words "reasonable and promising" are very subjective terms and are open to broad interpretation. Who's supposed to determine what's reasonable and what's promising? This is an important question that's not (but should be) answered in this contract. Due to the "Across The Board" deal nature of the Production Company's agreements with the artist, the management contract is co-terminus with the Exclusive Recording Artist Contract. Most managers argue that they need a two to three year initial term in order to develop a new artist's career to reach certain level of respectability. With this in mind, the artist's attorney should insist that more definite standards be incorporated into the contract obligating the manager to achieve a certain level of performance in order to have the right to extend the term into the option years. Achievements such as obtaining a recording agreement for the artist within the first year or helping the artist achieve minimum gross earnings in excess of a certain figure (i.e, $200,000 per year) should be required in order for the manager to earn the right to continue to represent the artist during the option years.

3. Most management contracts clearly state that the manager is not a booking agent and is not obligated to obtain employment for the artist. In certain

CONTRACT	ANALYSIS
any services which, standing alone, shall constitute Manager a talent agent, and Manager has not agreed or promised to perform such services except to the extent permitted by any applicable laws. Artist agrees to utilize proper talent or other employment agencies to obtain engagements and employment for Artist after first submitting the names thereof to Manager, and not to engage or retain any talent or other employment agency of which Manager may disapprove. Artist further agrees to submit all offers of employment (and all leads or other communications related thereto) and all contracts of any kind to Manager for Manager's advice and counsel and, if and to the extent permitted by applicable laws, approval.	states, regulations exist which prohibit managers from performing any services that may cause them to be deemed a talent agent. The states of New York and California have strict laws regulating talent agencies whose job is to procure employment for the artist. If a manager procures employment for the artist violating those regulations, they may be severely penalized. In California, for instance, a manager who provides the services of a talent agency but is not registered as a talent agent is acting in violation of the state's regulations. If this happens the artist may bring the manager before that state's labor commissioner who could terminate the management contract as well as order the manager to repay all commissions they may have earned during the term of the contract. Therefore, most managers take great pains to leave the procurement of employment to booking agencies licensed to perform this important function. The manager may, however, want the right to approve the booking agency and the terms of any agreement submitted to the artist before the artist's acceptance of such engagement.
4. (a) If Artist is, in the sole discretion of Manager, not reasonably available to execute any employment agreement (or related or similar written instrument) not requiring Artist's exclusive services for in excess of seven (7) full days, Manager may, at Manager's sole election, execute such agreement (or instrument) as	4. I feel that this paragraph is one of the most important clauses in any management contract because it grants the manager a power of attorney to act on the artist's behalf, particularly in situations where the artist's signature is needed. This power of attorney gives the manager the right to act on the artist's behalf. From my perspective as a lawyer and performer, I

CONTRACT

Artist's attorney-in-fact. Manager shall also be authorized, in Manager's discretion, on Artist's behalf, to approve and permit any and all publicity and advertising for Artist and to approve and permit the use of Artist's name, photograph, likeness, caricatures, voice and/or sound effects for the purposes of advertising and publicity and/or in the promotion of any and all products and services, and Artist shall not approve or permit any of the foregoing without Manager's approval thereof.

(b) (i) Artist hereby irrevocably appoints Manager as Artist's true and lawful attorney to collect and receive for Artist all compensation or other income or payments intended for Artist, which portion is payable to Manager hereunder (and Manager may deduct therefrom and retain any monies due Manager hereunder and/or deduct from any portion of such compensation, income or payments and pay therefrom any monies due any third party for any reason), as well as endorse, sign, make, execute and deliver all checks, drafts, notes and bills of exchange that may be drawn in Artist's name which are payable with respect to Artist's services and Artist hereby gives Manager the full power, right and authority to do any or all of the foregoing as Manager shall, in Manager's sole discretion, deem advisable in as full and ample a manner as Artist could do if personally present and Artist hereby

ANALYSIS

know this clause should be as narrowly limited as possible, only giving the manager the right to sign on the artist's behalf in special instances. In this contract, the manager is granted the power of attorney to sign contracts for performance engagements limited to seven (7) days or less. Any engagement less than seven days may be executed by the manager and will legally commit the artist to that engagement. However, a recording contract with a term of one year or a month long residency engagement in Vegas like the ones Santana, Celine Dion and Britney Spears have entered into recently, cannot be signed on the artist's behalf by the manager. This contract also grants the manager the power to approve all publicity and use of the artist's name and likeness for the promotion of various aspects of the artist's career. This provision also grants the manager the power to collect and receive all compensation intended for the artist, giving the manager the right to endorse checks made payable to the artist as well as sign checks drawn on the artist's bank accounts. The manager may also deduct their commission from the funds received on behalf of the artist. Should the artist receive any gross compensation directly, the artist is deemed to be holding such funds in trust for the manager and within forty-eight (48) hours of receipt the artist is required to transfer the funds to the manager. The artist also agrees to instruct any party from whom the artist expects to receive compensation, to pay the funds to the manager directly. The artist

CONTRACT

ratifies and confirms all that Manager shall do or cause to be done by reason thereof, except as may be otherwise expressly provided elsewhere in this Agreement.

      (ii) Notwithstanding any provision to the contrary contained herein, Manager shall not execute any recording agreements, motion picture agreements or any other agreement which will require Artist to render services for one (1) year or more without obtaining Artist's prior consent.

(c) In the event any gross compensation (as hereinafter defined) which should have been paid to Manager pursuant to the terms of this Agreement is nonetheless received at any time by Artist or by any other person, firm or corporation or other entity(ies) of any kind or nature on Artist's behalf, including, without limitation, any agent and/or business manager, same shall be deemed to be held in trust for Manager, and Artist shall immediately require the source of such gross compensation to thereafter conform to the provisions of this Paragraph 4 and shall, within forty-eight (48) hours of receipt of such gross compensation, remit or cause the remittance of all such gross compensation to Manager from the first monies so received and prior to the payment of any other monies, and a photocopy of this Agreement shall (and hereby does) serve as an irrevocable letter of direction,

ANALYSIS

shouldn't be in favor of this type of provision unless he or she has a lot of faith and trust in the manager. While it is my preference for the artist to be the first one to receive any compensation, and subsequently pay the manager their commissions, I understand the manager's desire to be "kept in the loop" regarding the payment of commissionable income. If the manager is the first point of receipt of the artist's funds, as is the case here, the contract should also have a time and method by which the manager must account to and pay funds due to the artist. Similarly, if the artist is the first point of receipt of compensation, he or she should be contractually obligated to pay the manager's commission in a prompt and timely manner. The artist also acknowledges in this paragraph that the manager is not required to make any loans or advances but, if the manager does so the artist agrees to repay the manager promptly.

    As I mentioned earlier, while the manager's agreement is exclusive to the artist, who can have only one manager, it is not exclusive to the manager, who may represent other artists during the term of this contract. This too is a provision the artist may try to limit if the artist feels that the manager may represent an act similar to and, as a result, in competition with the artist either at that time or in the future. The artist may therefore request a provision that limits the manager's right to represent other talents within the same category of music as the artist.

CONTRACT

authorizing and directing any and all other persons, firms and corporations or other entity(ies) to at all times so remit such gross compensation as provided above.

(d) Artist hereby warrants and agrees that any and all agreements entered into by, for or concerning Artist during the Term hereof (including any extensions and renewals thereof) shall provide for payment directly to Manager in accordance with the provisions of this Paragraph 4, and that Artist shall promptly execute and deliver to each other party to any such agreements already entered into an irrevocable letter of direction (in form acceptable to such party) effectuating the provisions of this Paragraph 4, and Artist further warrants and agrees that in the event any existing agreement is hereinafter amended, Artist shall cause such amendment, to include a provision for payment directly to Manager in the manner hereinabove set forth.

(e) Artist acknowledges that Manager is not required to make any loans or advances to Artist, but in the event Manager does so, Artist agrees to repay Manager promptly and Manager is hereby irrevocably authorized to deduct the amount of such loans or advances from any sums which Manager may receive for Artist's account.

5. Artist understands that Manager may also represent other persons

ANALYSIS

CONTRACT

and performers and that Manager's services hereunder are not exclusive. Artist agrees that Manager shall not be required to devote Manager's entire time and attention to fulfilling Manager's obligations under this Agreement, and that Manager shall have the right to render services to other persons, firms and corporations either in the capacity which Manager is employed hereunder or otherwise. Artist warrants that Artist will actively pursue Artist's career in the entertainment industry and will give due consideration to all advise and counsel proffered by Manager hereunder. Artist agrees at all times to be devoted to Artist's career and to do all things reasonably necessary to promote same.

6. (a) In full compensation for Manager's services hereunder, Artist shall pay to Manager, as and when received by Artist, or by Manager as provided herein, and prior to payment of any other party, twenty percent (20%) of the "gross compensation" ("Commission") of Artist, as hereinafter defined, received at any time on account of any and all activities in the entertainment and publishing industries except as specifically excluded from this Agreement. "Gross compensation", as used herein, shall mean the gross sums of money or other considerations (including, but not limited to, fees, salaries, earnings, royalties, residuals, advances, report and/or union fees, bonuses,

ANALYSIS

6. Industry observers have noticed over the years that it always seems that managers who take their commission on the artist's gross income inevitably end up in a conflict with the artist, whose earnings are based on net income. As the artist bears the enormous expense of maintaining its career, it usually ends up with only a fraction of what the manager makes. If the artist happens to be a group, the additional division of net income usually results in the act becoming jealous, resentful, and/or envious of the manager's rapid accumulation of wealth, while they're left with the daily task of working just to make ends meet, so to say. To avoid this eventuality, progressive managers may consider agreeing to other formulas regarding the commission

CONTRACT	ANALYSIS
proceeds of sales, leases or licenses, recording costs, gifts, shares of stock, partnership interests and amounts paid for packaged television, motion pictures and radio programs) directly or indirectly earned or received by Artist or Artist's heirs, successors and assigns, or earned, received or expended by anyone on Artist's behalf, from any professional activities of Artist (and/or derived from the use of Artist's experiences or talents and/or the results or proceeds thereof), whether as an actor, writer, composer, author, lyricist, singer, musician, performer, artist, designer, cameraman, technician, director, producer, supervisor, executive, consultant or as owner in whole or in part of any properties, or as a stockholder or owner in whole or in part of any other kind of proprietary interest in a production, publishing or other firm or entity of any kind, and whether for the rendition of the Artist's services or from the sale or other disposition of literary, dramatic or musical property or package radio or television program, or any rights therein or thereto, or any use of Artist's name(s) (including, but not limited to [Group Name] or any other group or professional names individually or collectively used at any time by any member or members of Artist, alone or with others), likeness or talents for advertising purposes or otherwise, without any exclusion or deduction whatsoever, including all sums earned by Artist	process. In the seventies, it was reported that the late Benjamin Ashburn, then manager of the group, The Commodores (when Lionel Richie was a member), agreed to be made a partner with the group, in essence becoming a "seventh" member of the six-man group as far as being compensated for his services, thereby increasing his earnings along with and at the same rate as the group's members. However in most instances a manager's commission may range from a low of 10% to a high of 20% or more depending on a number of factors that may include the manager's involvement in securing a record deal. The manager may, but is not obligated to, advance the artist funds for recording demonstration records. However, if a manager undertakes this responsibility (or what I consider to be a "monetary expression of faith" in the artist), he or she may rightfully request a higher commission of 20%. More established artists might be able to negotiate a lower commission in the 10%–15% range. In this contract the commission rate is applied against all gross income of the artist. Although for new artists, the commission is usually based on gross income, in some situations, certain items of gross income may be excluded before calculation of the commission. Usually this occurs in instances where the artist has more clout and in such a case, income that is used to offset definite expenses, such as recording costs, may be excluded before determining the commissionable income. Note that in this contract any shares of property or

CONTRACT	ANALYSIS
during the Term of this Agreement, and thereafter, under any employment or contract now in existence or entered into or negotiated for during the Term hereof, or under any extension, modification, addition or renewal of such contract or employment, regardless of when entered into, or under a substitute, directly or indirectly, for such contract or employment, including, without limiting the foregoing, a contract or employment with an employer or contracting party entered into within six (6) months of the termination of a previous contract or employment if such previous contract or employment is commissionable hereunder, and any and all judgments, awards, settlements, payments, damages and proceeds (whenever received) relating to any suits, claims, actions, proceedings or arbitration proceedings arising out of any alleged breach of non-performance by others of any portion of any contracts, engagements, commitments or other agreements referred to in this Paragraph 6, all of which regardless of when entered into, when performed and when effective. Any Commissions or other sums due Manager resulting from any and all such judgments, awards, settlements, payments, damages and/or proceeds relating to any such suits, claims, actions, proceedings or arbitration proceedings shall be computed after first deducting counsel fees and disbursements, and any counsel fees	stock paid to the artist as compensation is also deemed "income" and therefore subject to the manager's commission. An example of the importance of the inclusion of this type of provision in a contract occurred when hit rapper, Curtis Jackson (50 Cent) endorsed Vitamin Water. In addition to receiving a $5 million cash payment, Jackson also insisted on being compensated with shares of stock (5% of the shares) in the privately held company, Glaceau, that made the product. Well, when Glaceau was sold years later to Coca Cola, the value of Jackson's shares resulted in him earning $100 million from the deal. Under the terms of this contract the manager would be entitled to his or her portion of shares as a commission. So, don't think this sentence has no value. Of course, the manager would like the definition of commissionable income to be as broad as possible, while the artist's representative should attempt to narrow its scope as much as possible.

CONTRACT

and disbursements therefrom shall be paid by Artist. Notwithstanding anything to the contrary contained in this Agreement, as to any motion picture, phonograph record, film, tape, wire, transcription, recording or other reproduction of any of Artist's activities in the entertainment industries or resulting therefrom which is created in whole or in part during the Term hereof (or thereafter pursuant to an engagement, contract or agreement subject to Commission hereunder), Manager's Commission shall continue for so long as any of same are used, sold, leased, or otherwise exploited, whether during or after the Term hereof. Manager's Commissions shall, at Manager's option hereunder, apply to any monies paid to Artist by any employer of Artist as travel or living expenses in connection with any engagements, employment or agreement performed, secured or entered into by Artist.

(b) Expiration of the Term of this Agreement shall not affect Manager's right to receive Commissions for the full duration thereof with respect to agreements, engagements and commitments negotiated or entered into or renewed (in whole or in part) during the Term of this Agreement or any renewals or extensions thereof or substitutions therefore during or after the Term hereof. As used in this Agreement, "Artist" shall include any corporation, partnership,

ANALYSIS

CONTRACT	ANALYSIS
trust and/or other business entity of any kind or nature owned (partly or wholly) or controlled (directly or indirectly) by Artist or any members of Artist's family, and Artist agrees to cause any such corporation, partnership, trust and/or other business entity ("Firms") to enter into an agreement with Manager on the same terms as contained herein. Artist agrees that all gross monies or other considerations directly or indirectly earned or received by such Firms, in whole or in part, in connection with Artist's activities in the entertainment industry shall be subject to Commissions hereunder. Any agreement with each such Firm shall provide that such Firm has a right to furnish Artist's services on the terms and conditions set forth in this Agreement and the Firm shall become a signatory to this Agreement or one identical hereto. Artist shall (and hereby does) personally guarantee the obligations of any such Firm under this or any other agreement such Firm may have with Manager or any of Manager's affiliates. In the event Artist receives, as all or a part of Artist's compensation for activities hereunder, stock or rights to buy stock in any corporation or if Artist becomes the owner or packager of any entertainment property, regardless of the form of such ownership or packaging interest, the percentage compensation hereunder shall apply to such interest, and Manager shall be entitled to appropriate percentage of such interest. Notwithstanding	

CONTRACT

the foregoing, Commissions hereunder shall not apply to union "scale" income received by Artist in connection with services as a non-featured side musician appearing on recordings or personal appearances of other (featured) artists unless Artist serves in royalty-earning and/or proprietary, controlling, ownership or partnership capacity in connection with such services, appearance or recording.

7. All expenses, other than normal minimum office overhead expenses, incurred by Manager on behalf of Artist (including, without limitation, long distance telephone calls, messenger fees, transportation and expenses while travelling, and promotion and publicity expenses) shall be promptly paid or reimbursed to Manager by Artist. Unless made reasonably necessary due to circumstances substantially outside of Manager's control, Manager shall not incur any single such expense in excess of Three Thousand Dollars ($3,000.00) without Artist's prior approval. Neither Manager nor any individual affiliated with Manager shall be required to travel to meet with Artist at any particular time or place, provided, however, that if Manager or any such individual employee of Manager does travel on behalf of Artist, then the cost of such travel and any and all expenses relating thereto shall be promptly paid or reimbursed by Artist.

ANALYSIS

7. The manager shall be paid promptly or reimbursed for all expenses, other than normal office overhead expenses incurred on behalf of the artist. However, the manager should have a certain dollar limit (in this contract, it's $3,000, which, in my opinion, is high for a new artist) above which he/she must first obtain the artist's approval before spending. Usually, all costs of the manager's travel (1st class or coach?) and incidental charges are to be reimbursed, as well as telephone charges, copying and other reasonable business expenses incurred on the artist's behalf. I strongly urge the artist to insist that the manager document these expenses and submit such charges to the artist on a regular basis.

CONTRACT	ANALYSIS
Notwithstanding anything to the contrary continued in this Paragraph 7, if the presence of Manager or any such individual is required outside the metropolitan area of [Artist's City] or City of New York, Artist agrees that Artist will pay for the expenses incurred, such expenses to consist of first class living accommodations and requirements (including any and all tips and incidentals) and travelling expenses. All such expenses incurred on Artist's behalf are to be paid in advance from Artist's accounts and expense statements are to be turned in by Manager after each trip. Artist understands and agrees that Manager will not be able to turn in receipts for many of the expenses incurred by Manager in the course of doing Artist's business and therefor in such cases where Manager is unable to obtain receipts, Manager's statement to Artist in writing shall be deemed to be proof of such expense. In the event Manager has to entertain any individual or group of individuals anywhere in the world on Artist's behalf, Manager shall have the right to deduct such expenses as Manager incurs from Artist's accounts and in the event the accounts Manager holds for Artist are not sufficient to repay or advance the needed money to Manager, Artist shall promptly reimburse Manager or advance such money to Manager from the accounts of Artist that Artist holds upon Manager's request to Artist for such monies.	

CONTRACT

8. This Agreement shall not constitute a joint venture by or partnership between Manager and Artist, it being understood that Manager is acting hereunder as an independent contractor and that Manager may appoint or engage other persons or entities to perform any of the services required hereunder.

9. It is understood and agreed that Manager shall not be held in any way liable or responsible for any breach of contract or act or omission on the part of any person, firm or corporation with whom any engagement or contract of any kind is entered into by or for Artist for any reason.

10. Artist acknowledges that it is difficult to determine the amount and exact nature of services Manager must render hereunder at Artist's request. Accordingly, but without limitation of the foregoing, it is agreed that Manager shall not be deemed in breach of any Manager's obligations hereunder unless and until Artist shall give Manager written notice, by pre-paid certified mail, return receipt requested, of the precise breach alleged and Manager fails, within thirty (30) days after receipt of such notice, to cure the breach specified by Artist, but only if cure thereof within such period is reasonable in view of the nature thereof and Manager's other responsibilities and obligations. In the event that the said cure cannot reasonably be completed within

ANALYSIS

CONTRACT	ANALYSIS
thirty (30) days, then in such event Manager shall not be deemed in breach if Manager shall have commenced such cure in good faith within said thirty (30) day period.	
11. From time to time during the Term of this Agreement, Manager or other persons or entities owned and/or controlled directly or indirectly by Manager, or Manager's partners, shareholders, officers, directors and employees, whether acting alone or in association with others, may package an entertainment program in which Artist is employed as an artist, or may act as the entrepreneur or promoter of an entertainment program in which Artist is employed as an artist, or may employ Artist in connection with the production of phonograph records, or as a songwriter, composer, arranger or otherwise in connection with the creation of literary or musical works. Such activity on Manager's or their part shall not be deemed to be a breach of this Agreement or of Manager's fiduciary obligations and duties to Artist, and such activity shall not in any way affect Manager's right to Commissions hereunder in all instances except as hereinafter specifically provided. Manager shall not be entitled to Commissions from Artist in connection with any gross monies or other considerations derived by Artist from (i) any employment or agreement hereunder where Artist is employed or engaged by Manager or by any person, firm or	11. This paragraph is a very important part of this contract for the production company owner who, as a result of the relationship being across the board, is also the artist's co-publisher and manager. It says simply, if the manager owns a company which also has a contract with the artist for, among other things, recording or publishing, any income earned by the artist from these other ventures shall not be subject to the manager's commission. This clause may allow the production company/publisher/manager's "Across The Board" interests to be validated. It acknowledges that the production company's interest in recording and publishing, in addition to managing the artist, is not considered a breach of the manager's fiduciary duty. Once a manager enters into a contract with an artist, he or she undertakes a fiduciary obligation to put the artist's interest above all else, even the manager's interest. This obligation is at the heart of the manager/artist relationship and a provision such as this is inserted to document the manager's agreement not to "double dip" or profit from being the owner of businesses involved in the artist's recording and publishing activities while also commissioning the earnings of the artist in these areas. If a manager attempts to "double dip," the manager clearly is

CONTRACT

corporation owned or controlled by Manager, or by any of Manager's partners, shareholders, officers, directors or employees, in any capacity (including, without limitation, as the package agent for the entertainment program in which Artist is so employed or engaged, as Artist's music or literary publisher, or as Artist's record or promotion company); (ii) the sale, license or grant of any literary or musical rights to Manager or any person, firm or corporation owned or controlled by Manager.

12. This Agreement shall be deemed to have been made in the State of New York and its validity, construction, performance and breach shall be governed by the laws of the State of New York applicable to agreements made and to be wholly performed therein. Artist agrees to submit to the jurisdiction of the Federal or State courts located in New York City in any action which may arise out of this Agreement and said courts shall have exclusive jurisdiction over all disputes between Manager and Artist pertaining to this Agreement and all matters related thereto. Nothing contained herein shall constitute a waiver of any other remedies

ANALYSIS

protecting his or her interests first and not the artist's. If that's the case, an artist may ask a court to invalidate all agreements he or she has with the manager based on the theory of breach of the manager's fiduciary obligation to the artist. By inserting this provision in the management contract, the manager is agreeing not to commission the artist's income earned from companies in which the manager already has a financial stake. Therefore, the manager, who signs an artist "Across The Board," cannot commission recording, publishing or songwriter's advances or royalties and usually ends up being able to commission only the income generated by activities such as the artist's personal performances, endorsements and other non-record or publishing activities.

12. The parties have the right to have the agreement construed under the laws of a particular state. In most entertainment contracts, the parties agree to be bound under the laws of a state where a great deal of entertainment law court decisions or state regulations exist. New York and California are two of the most popular states in this regard. This agreement stipulates that the courts of the state of New York shall have jurisdiction of and be the proper venue for any disputes.

CONTRACT

available to Manager. Nothing contained in this Paragraph 12 shall preclude Manager from joining Artist in an action brought by a third party against Manager in any jurisdiction, although Manager's failure to join Artist in any such action in one instance shall not constitute a waiver of any of Manager's rights with respect thereto, or with respect to any subsequent action brought by a third party against Manager.

13. Artist hereby represents and warrants that Artist has not entered into any agreements or contracts which shall or do in any way interfere or conflict with Artist's obligations, promises and/or warranties hereunder and that Artist is free to enter into this Agreement, and Artist agrees to indemnify and hold Manager harmless from any loss, cost or liability (including reasonable attorneys' fees) as a result of any breach by Artist of any of Artist's representations, warranties or covenants contained herein, including, without limitation, the provisions of Paragraph 9 hereof.

14. The services rendered by Artist are special, unique and irreplaceable, and any breach or threatened breach by Artist of any of Artist's obligations hereunder may be enjoined temporarily or permanently without regard to and without limiting any other remedy that may be available to Manager.

ANALYSIS

CONTRACT

15. In the event Manager (or Manager's successors and/or assigns, if any) shall assign or otherwise transfer this Agreement or any of Manager's (or their) rights hereunder to any corporation, entity or partnership (which Manager shall only have the right to do provided that [Name of Key Person in Production/Management Company] is a shareholder, partner, or employee thereof) or in the event Manager shall delegate any of Manager's (or their) obligations hereunder, in whole or in part, to any party(ies) at any time comprising Manager or any corporation owned by Manager (or them) or any of such parties in whole or in part, such assignment shall be (and hereby is) approved and accepted and deemed to be a novation of this Agreement. Artist shall not have the right to assign any of Artist's rights or delegate any of Artist's obligations hereunder. Without in any way derogating from the preceding sentence, this Agreement shall inure to the benefit of and be binding upon each of the parties hereto and their respective successors, assigns, heirs, executors, administrators and legal and personal representatives.

16. Any notice given hereunder shall be sufficient only if mailed via certified mail, return receipt requested, postage prepaid, and if to Manager, addressed to Manager at the address hereinabove specified, with a copy to [Production/

ANALYSIS

CONTRACT

Management Company Attorney's Name and Address], and any other address(es) of which Artist has been given notice as provided herein, and if to Artist, at Artist's last known address(es) or the following address or any other address(es) of which Manager has been given notice as provided herein: [Artist's Attorney's Name and Address]. Any notice shall be effective as of the date three (3) days after mailing as aforesaid in the continental United States except for notices of change in address (which shall only be effective on receipt).

17. Nothing in this Agreement shall be construed so as to require the commission of any act contrary to law. Wherever there is any conflict between the provisions of this Agreement and any present or future statute, law, ordinance or regulation the latter shall prevail, but in such event the provision(s) of this Agreement affected shall be curtailed or limited only to the minimum extent necessary to bring it within the requirements of the latter. (The parties hereto do not intend by the foregoing sentence to imply the illegality, voidness or unenforceability of any term, provision or paragraph of this Agreement).

18. This Agreement sets forth the entire agreement between the parties hereto, and replaces and supersedes all other agreements relating to the subject matter hereof. This

ANALYSIS

CONTRACT

Agreement cannot be modified, altered, terminated or otherwise changed except by an agreement in writing signed by the parties hereto. In the event that any party hereto initiates litigation to enforce this Agreement, the party prevailing to the greater extent shall be entitled to recover reasonable attorneys' fees and costs reasonably incurred in connection with such litigation. No waiver of any provision of this contract or of any default hereunder shall affect Manager's rights thereafter to enforce such provision or to exercise any right or remedy in the event of any other default, whether or not similar.

19. If necessary in Manager's good faith opinion to ensure Manager of payments for Manager's services as provided herein, Artist agrees to deliver to Manager a written assignment of so much of Artist's compensation from any source as hereinabove agreed upon to be Manager's compensation, and if not so delivered to Manager, Manager is authorized to draw an assignment to Manager for such salary, execute the same in the name of Artist and collect therefrom with the same force and effect as though signed by Artist in person, or to require any party paying such compensation directly or indirectly to Artist to pay the same over to Manager, in which event this instrument or a copy thereof shall be authority for such employer to make such deductions and payment. All the terms and

ANALYSIS

19. In this paragraph the manager is allowed, in his or her "good faith opinion" to request the artist to assign the right to compensation to the manager. It further states if the artist fails to so assign this right, the manager is empowered to effect such an assignment on his or her own. What it means is that the manager may request to be the first point of receipt of funds paid for the artist's services, which enables the manager to protect his or her right to receive commissions.

CONTRACT

conditions of this Agreement shall be irrevocable, this Agreement constituting a contract and a power of attorney and creating an agency coupled with an interest.

20. Artist hereby expressly agrees that Artist will not at any time, without Manager's express written consent, exert or permit any third party to exert any of the powers herein granted to Manager so as to create any confusion or conflict of authority in the mind of any third person. Artist understands and agrees that Manager's interest and compensation under this Agreement shall be a continuing interest and shall not be revocable in any event or for any reason whatsoever for the term of this Agreement and any extension(s), renewal(s), replacement(s) or substitution(s) thereof, except only as specified in this Agreement.

21. Manager shall have the right to advertise and publicize Manager as Artist's exclusive personal manager and representative and Artist shall cooperate and assist Manager in securing written (and, if applicable, logo) credit as such wherever reasonably possible.

22. Artist acknowledges that no promises, representations or inducements have been made by Manager or on Manager's behalf, except as specifically set forth herein, and Artist further acknowledges that Manager's acceptance

ANALYSIS

CONTRACT

and execution hereof is in reliance on this fact.

23. Artist hereby represents, warrants and agrees that Artist shall cooperate fully with Manager in any and all of Manager's efforts to comply with any laws as same may apply to the manner in which Manager conducts Manager's management business generally and/or as it specifically pertains to Artist and/or the rendition of Manager's services hereunder. Artist hereby further agrees to negotiate with Manager in good faith regarding any and all amendments which may be required to be made to this Agreement in order to conform to the requirements of any laws and/or in order to continue the personal manager relationship created hereby. Artist hereby acknowledges that Manager has advised Artist that Manager shares common ownership with [Production Company's Name], the record company with whom Artist is simultaneously entering into a recording agreement. Manager has advised Artist and Artist hereby agrees to obtain independent legal counsel to negotiate with [Production Company's Name] and to represent Artist regarding Artist's activities with [Production Company's Name].

24. Manager shall be entitled (but in no event shall be obligated) to secure, in Manager's own name or otherwise and at Manager's expense, life, accident, health and/or

ANALYSIS

24. Most managers' contracts also contain a provision that allows the manager to obtain a life insurance policy on the artist and be named the payee should the artist meet an

CONTRACT

other insurance covering Artist, either independently or together with Manager or any party Manager designates being the sole beneficiary thereof and neither Artist nor Artist's estate shall have any right, title or interest in and to such insurance or any proceeds therefrom. Artist shall cooperate fully with Manager in connection with the obtaining of such insurance, if any, including, without limitation, by timely submitting to medical examinations and by completing any and all documents necessary or desirable in respect thereof.

25. (a) This Agreement shall apply to each member of Artist jointly and individually. Accordingly, whenever the word "Artist" is used in this Agreement, it shall mean, except as otherwise expressly provided, each member of Artist jointly and severally. In the event that any member of Artist engages in any activities in the entertainment or publishing industries separate and apart from Artist as a group, this Agreement shall nonetheless apply and all the terms and conditions of this Agreement shall be applicable to such activities.

(b) Artist represents and warrants that following the date hereof, no individual shall become a member of Artist or otherwise ("New Member") until Artist has obtained

ANALYSIS

untimely death. I generally resent these provisions because they give me cause to believe that an unscrupulous manager, at some point, may find it more beneficial to have the artist dead than alive. However, it is reasonable to believe that a reputable manager has a vested financial interest in the artist's continued ability to perform. It's been reported that Tony Bennett, the legendary performer who's in his eighties, is booked solid for performances two or three years in advance. Should he pass prior to fulfilling the engagements, his manager, who is also his son, would take a severe financial loss and therefore should be allowed to protect his interests with a life insurance policy on this important client.

25. If the artist is a group, the manager may also have legitimate concerns about who comprises the group. Therefore, a provision that binds members of the group, whether the group stays intact or disbands, is reasonable. If a member is replaced, a manager may also want the right to approve the replacement, who shall also be required to execute a similar contract with the manager.

CONTRACT

Manager's prior consent. In this connection (A) any such New Member shall be automatically bound by all of the terms and conditions of this Agreement as if such New Member had executed this Agreement on the date hereof, and (B) Artist shall cause each such New Member to execute and deliver to Manager any and all documents which Manager deems necessary or expedient to evidence the foregoing, including without limitation, any agreement with Manager containing the same terms and conditions set forth herein, but Manager's rights hereunder shall not be diminished by any such approved New Member's failure or refusal to execute such agreement.

(c) Each person leaving, or ceasing to perform with the group, for any reason whatsoever (i) shall be bound by all the terms and conditions of this Agreement as though said leaving member(s) individually executed this Agreement and (ii) shall relinquish all of his or her rights, of any nature whatsoever (including but not limited to trademark, servicemark, etc.) in the group name to the remaining persons comprising Artist. In the event this Agreement is terminated prior to the expiration date hereof, including any renewal or extension period for any reason whatsoever, as to any person designated herein as "Artist", such termination shall not affect the continuing force and

ANALYSIS

CONTRACT

validity of each and all other persons designated as "Artist" herein.

(d) In the event that any individual(s) at any time comprising Artist do not execute this Agreement, it shall nonetheless be binding upon the individual(s) who have at any time signed it (in counterparts or all on one copy) as if only such individual(s) were listed on the first and last pages hereof.

26. If and to the extent that "Artist" at any time refers in whole or in part to a female artist, the words used herein to designate such artist that have been used in the masculine gender shall be deemed to have been used in the feminine gender.

27. Artist specifically acknowledges that this Agreement is executed as an arm's length transaction, separate and apart from any fiduciary or other duty or obligation of any kind or nature which may be owed by Manager or any affiliate of Manager to Artist, and that Manager is under not such duty or obligation to Artist in connection with this Agreement, whether or not Manager or any affiliate or Manager now has or at any time had had any fiduciary or other relationship of any kind or nature with Artist. It is specifically understood and agreed that Artist is free to utilize separate, independent legal counsel to advise Artist with respect to the respective rights and obligations of each party under this

ANALYSIS

CONTRACT

Agreement, any failure by Artist to seek or obtain such legal counsel to be Artist's sole choice (and contrary to Manager's wishes).

IN WITNESS WHEREOF, the parties hereunder set their hands and seals on the day and year first above written.

[Name of Management Company]

_____
An Authorized Signer

_____
Artist

IMPORTANT LEGAL DOCUMENT—CONSULT YOUR OWN ATTORNEY BEFORE SIGNING

ANALYSIS

15

Statement and Analysis of Management Earnings
Maximizing the Earnings of the Artist

In order to provide an effective analysis of management earnings, it is necessary to base the analysis on the activities of a fictitious artist. Let's suppose the artist is multitalented. He or she has a unique look or style that is attractive to certain product endorser's ("endorsements"), produces music for other artists as well as themselves ("third-party producer activities"), and is in demand for live performances ("live performances") and appearances in movies ("movie roles"). As a result, the artist is capable of generating income from at least four different sources in addition to his or her recording and songwriting activities.

Once the performer is signed with the production company, who also acts as the performer's manager in an across the deal arrangement, the management division of the production company cannot commission the artist's earnings from recording, songwriting, or publishing activities. However, if the artist is contracted for lucrative endorsements, third party producer activities, live performances, and movie roles, the earnings generated by these activities may be subject to commission by the manager.

In our model, we will deal with four types of artist activities where the earnings of the artist could be commissioned.

LIVE PERFORMANCES

First, if the artist has a successful record, it is likely she or he will obtain live performance engagements. If the artist performs 50 engagements at a fee of $5,000 per date, the manager will be entitled to $50,000 in commissions.

Artist's Gross Earnings	Management Commission (20% of Gross)
Artist performs fifty (50) dates at $5,000 per date 50 × $5,000 = $250,000 gross	$50,000

THIRD-PARTY PRODUCER ACTIVITIES

Second, if the artist produces five master recordings for $15,000 per recording for other acts not signed to the production company, the manager's commission on the $75,000 of income will be $15,000.

Artist's Gross Earnings	Management Commission (20% of Gross)
Artist/producer produces five (5) master recordings (sides) for parties other than the production company at $15,000 per side 5 × $15,000 = $75,000 gross	$15,000

ENDORSEMENTS

As a result of the artist's unique look and popularity, the manager is able to arrange an agreement with a toothpaste company, who wants to use the artist in national radio or TV/Internet commercials promoting their product. The deal calls for the payment of a fee of $100,000 to the artist. Of course, the manager's 20% commission amounts to $20,000.

Commissioned Activity	*Management Commission*
Artist endorses product (toothpaste commercial) One-time payment of $100,000	$20,000

MOVIE ROLES

If the artist has some acting talents, it is possible for the manager to arrange for his or her appearance in a motion picture. This medium is becoming increasingly popular for recording artists. While the fee for a cameo appearance or a featured role can range from $75,000 to $1 million, depending on the leverage of the artist, the time it takes to perform in a movie may have to be scheduled so it does not interfere with the artist's recording or live performance schedule. In our case, let's suppose the artist makes a featured performance in a movie for a flat fee of $100,000. In addition to providing both the artist and the manager with important earnings beyond recording and publishing, the exposure of the artist can greatly enhance his or her image as well as promote the artist's musical career.

Artist's Gross Earnings	*Management Commission (20% of Gross)*
Artist performs featured role in a motion picture One-time flat fee of $100,000	$20,000

While I vehemently decry and protest the recent changes in recording agreements as I alluded to earlier, which make it almost impossible for the artist to earn anything other than advances for recording services, the potential for earnings from the exploitation of the artist's other talents is enhanced by the success of record sales/streaming and should not be overlooked.

In today's popular culture, where any publicity is considered good publicity, artists who achieve success in music will find themselves in a great position to generate additional earnings from other sources such as advertisers, movie companies, clothing manufacturers, liquor companies and so on.

You see from this example that a successful artist should strive to generate income from as many sources as benefit the development of his or her career. An exceptionally talented artist can become a multi-faceted, self-sustaining business entity, generating substantial income for both themselves and their manager.

16

Live Performance
Having It, Working It, Making It

Live performance is the main breadwinner for most artists these days. As a result of tremendous growth of festivals like Loolapalooza, Coachella, Ultra and events like SXSW that feature music ranging from Rock and Country to EDM, the live performance market has grown significantly since the beginning of this century. Part of that growth is attributable to an expanding international market place for these types of events. International festivals like Primavera Sound in Spain, Roskilde in Denmark and Fuji Rock in Japan have routinely been ranked in the world's top-ten best festivals. At the time of this writing, some leading live promotion companies are not only experiencing record breaking revenue, attendance and ticket sales but expect the boom times to extend well into the emerging digital age, as fans link with artists and ticket-buying opportunities via various services like YouTube, iRadio, Spotify and others.

Being a vibrant live performer is a unique art form that takes years to master, but pays dividends that can last a whole career. Take for instance my former clients, The O'Jays, who first formed with five members as teenagers in the late 1950s. At that time, they decided to build an audience by offering a unique live performance experience—combining excellent vocals with exciting, precision choreographic moves that would engage each audience they appeared before. As a result of adopting this approach, they went on to become fan favorites, Rock & Roll Hall of Fame inductees and still perform today, selling out halls and auditoriums wherever they appear.

THE *IT* THEORY

Having "It"

In order to become a successful live performer you first must have *it*. "It" is that mysterious, unexplainable ability to captivate an audience's attention with your talent. You may have overheard someone singing a song that stopped you in your tracks and made you say, "What a great voice! You certainly have *it*!" Some people call this quality the "X Factor" and the producers of the television show of the same name say that the title refers to the indefinable "something" that makes for star quality. Someone first told me I had it when I was in high school. One of the members of a vocal group, The Illusions, I was managing couldn't sing a lead line of a Temptations song, where the great David Ruffin does an octave jump from tenor to a falsetto voice in the first phrase of "I Could Never Love Another, Like I'm Loving You" (check it out on a streaming service). When I stepped in to show him and hit the phrase perfectly, the other group members insisted I should not only manage, but perform in the group as well. Not everybody has "it," but for those who do, having it doesn't mean that you're going to be successful in your music career. You can have "it" but to become successful you not only have to *have* it, you must *work* it!

Working "It"

The Illusions, a five-man vocal group of high school classmates, performed at school talent shows, community luncheons, banquets and other functions throughout the Cleveland, Ohio area. We never got paid, but just enjoyed the opportunity to display and hone our talents. Soon word spread (word of mouth is one of best forms of promotion) and our performance calendar became busier. We worked whenever and wherever we were asked to make an appearance. We even made our own record (that's right, a record, not a tape, CD or Download), giving me my first experience in a recording studio. I was working it!

At Syracuse University (SU) where I went to college, my then college roommate, the late Eddie Hines and I started a band with a group of upperclassmen. The band, "The Decade" was our platform for making a little money and developing our sound and performing skills. For the next two years we worked Frat and Sorority parties on weekends. After the upperclassmen graduated, Eddie and I decided to form a new group and auditioned singers from the local community. After discovering tremendously talented singers and musicians and changing the group name to "The New Decade", we decided that we wanted to not only work on the SU campus, but also nightclubs in Syracuse and beyond . . . and that's just what we did. We practiced relentlessly and performed first in the Syracuse area and, as word of our dynamic show spread, began performing at clubs and colleges in neighboring cities in upstate New York, including Rochester, Buffalo, Utica, Rome and Albany. As of result of meeting other traveling bands on the road, we were put in contact with a booking agent that arranged for us to tour Canadian cities like Halifax and Toronto. In other words, we put in the work that, in addition to building our prowess as musicians and entertainers, also created important contacts that enabled us to build both an audience and a network of other musicians and industry professionals, all of which would come in handy in the future.

Making "It"

After over five years of working it with The New Decade, I decided to move to New York City to pursue my goal of recording for a nationally distributed record label. After working "it" for over five years, I was ready to make it. The first night I was in New York my first phone call was to Larry Blackmon, the leader of the group Cameo, a group that had performed in many of the same cities the New Decade performed in. Larry and I had mutual respect for each others' talent and desire to become successful entertainers. The conversation went something like this, "Hey Larry, I moved to NYC and I'm ready to sing." His response was immediate and welcomed. He said, "Great, we're going into the studio to cut demos tonight, come on by." I did and ended up recording the lead and background falsetto vocals on most of Cameo's first album, "Cardiac Arrest," nationally distributed by Casablanca Records, the label that also had the number-one single at the time, "Love to Love You Baby" by Donna Summer. I learned a very important lesson from this experience. It's not enough to have "it." If you have "it," you must work "it." If you have "it" and work "it" you can make "it!"

Having a dynamic live show is one of the most important aspects of developing a long and fruitful relationship with your audience. You can create awareness through a trending YouTube video and SoundCloud streaming experience, but in my estimation, an engaging live performance is the glue that cements the fan relationship. It takes time to develop a show that captivates an audience and makes them want to support you in your endeavors . . . a show you know will generate a standing ovation. Some artists like U2, Imagine Dragons, Rolling Stones, connect with audiences as a result of incorporating great musicianship, vocals and production features into their shows. Others like Jennifer Lopez, Pit Bull and the aforementioned O'Jays, Beyonce, Katy Perry, Justin Timberlake, Usher, Chris Brown and Justin Bieber all employ choreographic moves that work to excite the crowd. But movement and intricate production details are not the only way to elicit a standing ovation. Sometimes just the virtuosity of an artist's talent can captivate an audience. Adele, Wayne Shorter, Marc Anthony, McCoy Tyner, and Gregory Porter are all artists whose sheer power of their talent can command this type of response as well. Developing the art of performing live is time extensive.

Sometimes it can take years to learn how to effectively engage a live audience. They used to call it "paying your dues," when artists worked years on the road learning the craft of pleasing an audience. However, in our current instant Internet everything world, many artists spend too much time recording and not enough time putting together a show stopping live set. A live show producer once told me a story about a band he was coaching. The band told him that, while they spent a year and half recording an album that only generated 10% of their yearly income, they only spent a week preparing their live show from which they generated over 80% of the money the band earned each year. That's putting the cart before the horse, don't you think? So, be sure to put the requisite amount of time and energy needed to develop a great live show.

I fondly remember seeing the O'Jays rehearse their act with their choreographer, the late Cholly Pops"Atkins, a renowned member of the tap dance duo "Coles and Atkins" in the 1940s. Atkins decided to enter the new field of coaching young Doo-wop singing groups in the 1950s and would eventually work with The O'Jays. The O'Jays would rent a hotel room for over a month and rehearse five-six hours a day learning Atkins' intricate, unparalleled choreographic moves that set them apart from any other vocal group of their time. The routine he developed for his initial client, the vocal group The Cadillacs, was so dynamic—with synchronized steps and energetic moves, that his reputation grew rapidly, and by the 1960s he became the in-house choreographer for all the great Motown acts. We owe Pops a debt of gratitude for developing what has now become the staple for all Pop acts that use multiple dancers in the background (and sometimes foreground) of their performance routines.

Recording is a different art that requires an artist to spend a significant amount of time in recording studios learning how to transfer the emotion they emit from their stage performance to a new setting: a vocal recording booth with no audience around to spur them on. The only way to perfect the art is to record whenever and wherever possible. Gerald Levert's father, Eddie Levert produced his first recordings. As a result of Eddie's persistent coaching, Gerald was able to achieve a consistent sound on his first few recordings. But it wasn't until several years later when Gerald decided to spend hours everyday in the recording studio that he really developed his own sound . . . a sound that made him one of the all-time great recording artists. Recording is no longer a breadwinner, but an attention-getter.

Once you have the attention, the live performance is the adhesive that cements a long-lasting relationship with fans that can be maintained by ongoing communication with fans through a steady stream of social media outlets like Face book, Twitter, etc. The artist/fan relationship isn't just about money, but support as well. Indie artist Amanda Palmer is a believer that this timeless relationship is about acknowledging the presence and worth of the individual. After developing a following through Twitter and other social media outlets over the years, she was able to raise over a million dollars through a Kickstarter campaign by offering various levels of rewards to fans, who supported her effort in recording a new album and subsequent tour. Her rewards not only included copies of the CD, but opportunities for those pledging certain dollar amounts to have special fan experiences, like a performance in their homes, etc. On her tour she often tweeted that she needed a place for her and her band to stay when they were in a certain town. Her fans would open the doors to their homes to her and the band . . . offering not just lodging but meals as well, in a show of support of Amanda's dedication to her art. Fans want to support not only the recordings and live performances of the artist, but also unique experiences with the artist. Once this type of relationship is developed and nurtured, fans will support all endeavors of an artist, including purchasing merchandise of both the artist and any products or services the artist endorses or sponsors.

> Once you have the attention, the live performance is the adhesive that cements a long-lasting relationship with fans.

17

The Evolving Digital Age
From the Ground to the Cloud

Since the turn of the century, the recording industry has faced several issues resulting from the transition of analog audio/visual recordings to the digital format. Digital recording's near-perfect duplication of sounds and images has resulted in widespread piracy of copyrighted works. In the early 2000's, software providers Napster, Kazaa, and Grockster allowed (and many would say, encouraged) users to trade millions of unauthorized copyrighted works through peer-to-peer file sharing (P2P) decimating the of earnings of music creators and their affiliated companies. While entertainment is still a multi-million dollar industry and a major force in the U.S. economy, losses created by P2P file sharing and other forms of piracy have left many major and independent record labels reeling in red ink, forcing consolidation on an unprecedented scale. What was once the Big Six record labels in the 1990s have been, as of the date of publishing this edition, reduced to the Big Three (SONY, Universal Music Group and Warner Music Group), as a result of the 2012 purchase of the recording and publishing assets of EMI by Universal Music Group and SONY/ATV, respectively. Record sales plummeted in spite of successful lawsuits brought by the industry trade group, Recording

Industry Association of America (RIAA) against various service providers (i.e., Napster and Kazaa) and individual users. Since P2P file-sharing site Napster emerged in 1999, yearly record sales in the U.S. have dropped 56 percent, from $14.6 billion to $6.4 billion in 2012. Experts estimate continued declines of 1.3% over the next five years to $6B in 2017.

Record companies still generate a significant portion of their revenue from the sale of albums, but the return of the industry having a healthy singles market (either downloaded or streamed) creates a new paradigm that challenges songwriters, artists, record, publishing and production companies in several ways. Although record companies are experiencing revenue growth from new sources like digital single sales, sound recording performance royalties and synchronization uses, it still isn't enough to offset the loss of income resulting from lower album sales. Artists, songwriters and their respective production and publishing companies are also experiencing reduced earnings in the current singles market. Artist royalty rates for singles may be only 75% of album royalty rates and, as the sale price for singles is substantially lower than for albums, an artist has to sell significantly more singles to account for the loss of earnings occasioned by a continuing reduction in album sales. In addition to reduced artist royalty earnings as a result of consumers purchasing singles instead of albums, record companies are also reducing the amount of advances they give artists.

Songwriters and publishers concerns about a change of business model that focuses on singles as opposed to albums sales as well. Whereas, in the not too distant past, an artist-songwriter who wrote a number of songs on an album could expect mechanical royalties for each song from the sale of a substantial amount of albums, now they must instead hope for a significant increase in the number of single sales in order to achieve comparable level of earnings from this important source of revenue.

The synchronization of master recordings and compositions from the audio medium to the video medium is also a growing source of revenue to record companies and publishers alike. Every time a hit record you've heard on the radio is subsequently used in a television show, movie or commercial, the rights to do so must be obtained from the record company and/or publisher of the compositions. However, the use of music for video continues to grow at such a frenetic pace, many master and composition copyright owners are finding that an oversupply of works in the marketplace is reducing the amount of fees they can command for such uses.

However, in the 2003 book, The Future of Music, authors, Dave Kusek and Gerd Leonhard predicted future generations would, at some point, eschew the purchase and owning of recorded music and choose instead to access music through various streaming music services. Although it has taken a while for this concept to gain traction, it appears that more music consumers have bought into the authors' "music like water" model and either use free or subscription Internet outlets like Rhapsody, YouTube, Pandora, Spotify, iRadio or Rdio to enjoy their music. Streaming music from one or more of these services appears to have caught the eyes, ears and minds of millions of music lovers and it appears that the "all access as opposed to ownership" model may, over time, reach the potential espoused in the book.

The live performance market also is experiencing massive growth as a result of greater promotional opportunities available for artist exposure in the digital space. Live performances may be the primary income generating activity of an artist's career. Many artists depend on gigs to provide the bulk of their income. The Future of Music Coalition (FMC) is a non-profit organization that educates and advocates for the rights of musicians and consumers in an effort to create a middleclass of musicians. The ability of an artist to create a community of fans that support their creative work is greatly enhanced by opportunities to be discovered and supported through various low (or no) cost digital means. An artist that trends on YouTube, Facebook, Twitter and the like, may use additional digital services like Spotify, Sonicbids, Eventful.com and others to create a market for their live performances in a heretofore, unheard of way.

The digital age promises to be both a frightening and exciting time for the growth of music. As digital technology matures and music business models change, there may be more outlets for and revenue generated from music than ever before. However, as music business opportunities for revenue growth expands, it is important for all interested parties including songwriters, publishers, recording artists and record companies to agree on equitable ways of sharing in the revenue to insure that they all are able to earn a sufficient livelihood from creating this great work.

18

Incorporating the Information

Some might consider the first part of this book the easy material. You've gone through the contracts and reviewed the analysis. Hopefully, you've gotten an answer to a question that's puzzled you for a while and maybe even caused procrastination or problems. You've read and reread about the importance of applying keys for success, the Three Big P's, structuring the relationship of the players involved, and details about people in the business. Now it's time to take what you've read and begin to incorporate the information into your business frame and frame of mind.

Whether you're about to begin your business or are in the process of reorganizing now is the time to apply the information and make it work for you. Reread the section on choosing the proper business structure. If you have questions, write them down and meet with a professional who is qualified to give you answers. Yes, it will cost you. But the cost of charges for a professional (an attorney or accountant) in the early stages of your career to get advice is miniscule when compared with the amount of time and earnings that can be lost (or not flowing to your account!) if your contracts are not designed to work in your best interest. Having the right foundation can make the difference in both the short and long run. Make certain you have your business plan written down so that your focus is clear to you and anyone you intend to do business with. The contracts are there for you to review at any time—that's why you bought the book. Take the time to do a mental review and think about how to adapt the basic structures to your situation. Again, if you have questions, seek advice. Remember, the contracts are samples and should be used only as guidelines to what is going on in the legal end of the music business. Don't do yourself a disservice by trying to evaluate and make actual changes or assume that you will be able to apply them to your particular situation. It may appear simple, but as I've pointed out earlier, the fine print is not to be taken lightly—remember, your business is at stake and the stakes in this business are high.

When you meet with your professional advisers or your partners or if you choose to work independently while you are structuring your business, keep in mind the importance of diversifying your income. Take advantage of the available markets (mutual funds, stocks, IRAs, etc.). Find out what's available and get your money involved to work for your future while your music is working for you now and in the future.

I have to reiterate the importance of education. Read, read, read. Know what's going on in the entertainment business and in the world. You'll be surprised to find out how closely related all movements in business in general impact the music business.

As you read the last section of this book, keep in mind that it encapsulates situations and ideas. Read through these last pages and be ready to move your business forward and create the best of times in the music industry.

19

Moving You and Your Business into the Future

We've finished the review of the contracts and the general concept of how to take care of your business. Now it's time to understand how to move forward with strategies for success for your future in the music business.

The truly talented can make a living in the music industry if they have perseverance and determination. Take, for example, the major talents I've associated with over the years; two I represent and one I've performed with. Each one has been a true testament to my belief. In the late 1960s, the O'Jays lived around the corner from my childhood home in Cleveland, Ohio, with one of their relatives. The neighborhood was great, but it wasn't the music capitol of the world. Times were hard in the record business and I'm sure The O'Jays—like the rest of us—were having a difficult time making ends meet. But they persevered and captivated audiences at the legendary Leo's Casino in Cleveland, the Uptown in Philly, and the Regal in Chicago. Wherever they performed they made their smooth love song, "Look Over Your Shoulder," and the dance hit, "One Night Affair," come alive in the hearts and minds of the audience. In 1971, Gamble & Huff signed The O'Jays to their Philadelphia International Records label (which was distributed by Columbia Records and run, at that time, by Clive Davis). They saw to it The O'Jays got their just due and the hit records started with "Backstabbers" and "Love Train" and continued with "Used to Be My Girl" and "For the Love of Money."

Then there was Larry Blackmon. Years before there was Cameo, Larry had a group called The New York City Players. They played on what was commonly referred to in the business as the "chitlin' circuit," which was a small network of clubs in the United States and Canada that featured, on a weekly basis, predominantly black performing acts. The "circuit" was a grind but it kept the groups busy and on bus tours in order to make dates. My group, The New Decade, made the tour as well until I joined Cameo shortly after it was formed in 1976. It was during my brief work with Larry's group that I made the decision to get a law degree in order to best protect and advance my musical career. The demands of law school kept me from being a part of the eventual musical success I knew had to and would happen for Cameo (because Larry had overdrive!) but I moved forward with no regrets. With hard work and determination, success occurred for them in a huge way in 1987 with their international hit, "Word Up."

Lastly, I have to mention the late, great Gerald Levert. Many people probably think he had it made because of his father, Eddie Levert, lead singer of The O'Jays. What people don't know is that it took two years of performing in small clubs, writing songs, and perfecting his skills while he was still in high school. During that time, his group, Levert, released an album on Network Records, an independent record label owned by Harry Coombs, former VP of Marketing for Philadelphia International Records. The group was soon signed by Hank Caldwell, VP of Black Music at Atlantic Records and had their first hit, "Pop, Pop, Pop Goes My Mind." Gerald went on to become the premiere songwriting, producing and performing male vocalist of his era before his untimely death in 2006.

Each of these people all had talent and I know they wouldn't have survived without powerful product, proper perspective, and professional attitude (Determination helped quite a bit, too!)—all factors necessary for achieving complete success in today's music industry.

Having grown up during the era of "soul music" and "funk" bands, I was influenced and inspired by tremendous songwriters and performers such as Curtis Mayfield, Marvin Gaye, and Stevie Wonder, and I can personally affirm the inspirational qualities of music. I contend, at least from my experience, that "people gotta have it"—"it" being music that moves the body and the soul, confirming my belief that music has been and will always be a primary source of spiritual uplift and social entertainment for the masses.

In the new millennium, the scope and breadth of the entire entertainment business will increase exponentially. Commentators have already noted the effect entertainment is having on all businesses in general. In these times everyone wants to be entertained in some form or fashion, during his or her every waking hour. I've seen music become totally pervasive: there's mood music in stores to encourage sales from the hip-hop beats on high volume in the sneaker section, to the sensuous love melodies for choosing lingerie. Even the most staid banking and financial institutions are attempting to "lighten up" by incorporating certain aspects of entertainment into their marketing schemes. Have you noticed the new cartoon graphics on many of the ATM machines you use? You can bet you'll soon be hearing a hip-hop audio-track to accompany these exciting visuals. It makes taking money out (and depleting your balance) an experience you're more apt to enjoy with the excitement of music. So what does this say to the individual with creative musical or other talents? It says—loud and clear, confirming what I know to be true—these are great times to be in this business. While Internet streaming and the shift to the access model from the physical (CD/download buying) model is rapidly taking hold, I believe it won't be long until most consumers subscribe to music services that allow them access to any and all recordings at any time. When that occurs, and I believe it will before the next decade, more revenue will be available for all participants in the music industry (Internet service providers, record and publishing companies, artists and songwriters) to be fairly compensated for their contribution to bringing great music to the world.

For the creative person the future holds the potential to provide unlimited wealth and success. However, just as in the past, having knowledge of how the business works is essential, but it is not always enough. You not only have to know how to TCB (Take Care of Business), you also have to be dedicated to knowing how to SIB (Stay in Business). As the business world changes be confident that you can change with it. Everyone should learn and apply new skills and be able to step in at a moment's notice to do a job no one thought could be done. The ability to TCB and SIB will be even more promising if you understand and apply the Three Big P's and recognize their importance in the future of the ever-growing and ever-changing entertainment business.

POWERFUL PRODUCT AND THE FUTURE

Powerful product will be just as important in the future as it is now, not only as background music for ATM graphics or selling merchandise in department stores and online, but also as a tool to generate revenue for the artist's share of the millions of dollars that can be gained from worldwide Internet record streaming. Business will be changing hands in a New York second with people in all realms of business creating powerful products and knowing how to exploit them. Each change will come at the speed of the fastest computers and their streaming and downloading capabilities. We'll find more often that artists will be reaching (and selling products and services in) China, Paris, and Mexico with their fans hitting "Enter" on the keyboard.

For those in the music industry, the focus in the future is not only on the powerful products created but also the effect of new technological innovations that will provide access to these products and services. This means you have to be able to cross-promote. In order to do this, creative talent must develop a synergistic approach to the exploitation of talent through various media outlets; a recording artist, for example, could consider creating another powerful product by honing acting skills, a lyricist might want to investigate writing screen plays, and record producers could try their hand at producing and directing movies and television shows. A number of recording stars, such as Carrie Underwood, Katy Perry and Justin Beiber are already continuing the pattern set by earlier recording stars like Brandy, Ice Cube, and Dolly Parton each of whom knew the importance of SIB. Those artists mastered their "acting chops" for important cross-promotional activities in motion pictures and TV.

It's also important for recording stars to note the success of artists like rap star, Queen Latifah and singer Jewel, who not only perform on records, but also, star in movies, write books, and, in the case of Queen Latifah, develop and star in daily talk show. For Latifah, all this is in addition to running a successful movie and television show production company. She is definitely focused on creating a totally synergistic plan to TCB and SIB! Another paradigm is the Broadway production, Motown-the Musical, produced by Motown founder Berry Gordy and adapts the great Motown/Jobete Publishing treasure trove catalog of hit songs from the Motown era for the Broadway stage. Gordy's done what I call "morphing," being able to move from one career (record label founder) to another (Broadway producer), which is in my opinion, the key to SIB. Is the opportunity there? You bet. What you have to do in order to succeed is think of your business (yourself) as a product that can transform and restyle with time, while creating current and future earnings.

There is no doubt that changes will inadvertently make taking care of your music business easier because of the introduction of new and effective technological advancements that have been developed in recent years. Each of these advances will greatly enhance an artist's ability to create and exploit her or his powerful product. One major change has already occurred with the reduction in the price of (and the increase in the widespread use of) computers with recording capability. This alone has drastically cut the costs of recording and has enhanced the recording capability for many artists who were not able to afford expensive studio rates and the cost of hiring live musicians. While, in some genres, there currently seems to be a backlash against artists whose recordings are composed solely of synthesized sound, the use of live musicians (other than rhythm sections) is more likely a thing of the past. When you consider the high quality of computer-generated sounds, which provide horn and string accompaniment rivaling those created by real musicians, it's easy to understand why this process has been so readily embraced by one of the fastest growing music genres, Electronic Dance Music (EDM).

KEEP YOUR PROPER PERSPECTIVE FOR THE FUTURE

As previously mentioned, consolidation is another phenomenon occurring in the entertainment industry. Not only is it having a major effect on the music industry as it relates to record companies, it is also affecting the live performance market. Live Nation is one company that has emerged as a major "consolidator" in the area of concert promotion and venues. At the time of this writing, Live Nation owns, or operates under lease, over a hundred venues, including a number of amphitheaters in the top ten U.S. live performance markets. It's chief rival, the Anschutz Entertainment Group (AEG) operates in a similar manner, owning several prime venues across the world. Live Nation also merged with Ticketmaster, the world's leading ticket-seller, creating an organization that dominates the worldwide live performance market. Over the past few years, Live Nation has purchased most of the large concert promoters in the United States. It's most recent surge has been in the Electronic Dance Music (EDM) market, where the company has expanded its holdings in EDM live promotion companies, ticketing agencies and festivals and, as a result, increased its overall revenue by 8.3% in 2013. As indicated in an article from *Newsweek* magazine years ago, "No single company has ever controlled so much of the live entertainment business." The venture has caused many smaller promoters and booking agencies to express concern about the future of the live performance business. These promoters contend that the control exerted by Live Nation leases on venues throughout the country will lessen their ability to present shows in the most desirable concert halls and auditoriums. There are also the surviving independent booking agents who fear that Live Nation will (because of its power to approach live performers directly with the promise of a nationwide prepackaged tour in its venues) undercut and eliminate the need for their services.

Artists have valid concerns that a company with the control of Live Nation may eventually be able to dictate the price they receive from large tours by arguing "either you tour with us at X [their dollar] amount or you can't perform in our venues." This is a real problem for many artists because they know live performance revenue is their primary source of income. However, the upside to Live Nation's focus on the superstar act touring business is that it may create a more positive environment for the lesser-known niche market acts smaller promoters and venues will undoubtedly be craving for in order to fill their live performance calendars. Artists with the foresight and determination to deliver good, solid, live performances can and will be appreciated by the national audiences they'll build from touring small clubs through local promoters. As always, he or she who controls the powerful product will control his or her own destiny. The popular alternative country and folk rock singer-songwriter, Brandi Carlile, for example, built her growing audience over the years from humble beginnings working coffee shops in her hometown of Seattle. She toured small clubs at first but, after the release of her first album in 2004, had the opportunity to open for The Fray on their tour of several House of Blues venues across the U.S. As a result of seeing her perform at the Cleveland HOB, I became a fan and, over the years, she has built a career that has enabled her to headline at 10,000 seat venues like Denver's Red Rocks amphitheater.

You must also recognize that what were once the standard avenues of doing business, are not being eliminated but are merely changing to meet the challenges of a new era. Consolidation and the resulting downsizing of major record labels has had a profound effect on the music business and forced everyone involved to develop (if they haven't by now) the "proper perspective." These two factors alone (consolidation and downsizing) have resulted in the narrowing of opportunities to affiliate with major record labels not only for the artists, but also for record company executives. Many will be forced to outline survival tactics to get them through. The change is in full swing, with the foundations of the recording industry giving way to new structures.

In 2012 the "Big Four" was reduced to the "Big Three," as the Universal Music Group (UMG) purchased EMI's recorded music arm for $1.9 billion. This created the largest record company in the world. Universal Music Group recorded revenues of $3.66 B in the first half of 2013—up 16.3% period on period. Digital sales for the label represented 53% of recorded music sales in the half compared to 47% in 2012. It's the first time the company has seen digital account for more than half of overall sales.

It has been reported that the UMG and EMI consolidation of operations led to significant cost savings. This brilliant business move resulted in a leaner and meaner company, with fewer acts (*read:* fewer opportunities for new developing acts) and a reduced executive roster. Its been said that major record labels commit at least $1 million for each new artist album release. This cost includes recording, manufacturing, distribution, and promotion. If the act doesn't sell at least 250,000 units, it may not be profitable for the major label to commit to recording another of the artist's albums.

The culprit driving the major labels' need to sell a million in order to make millions is high overhead. While the double-edge sword of digital-age recording technology drastically reduces the actual costs of recording, it also allows major labels to use this argument to justify lower advances to artists to record their albums—a trend that has been accelerated upon completion of the consolidation process of the major labels, as the opportunities for new artist contracts are few and far between.

With the upheaval of the well-established recording giants, some in the industry are in a panic. Then there are those of us who know there will always be a target market for various genres of music and money to be made for now and the future.

DON'T MISS YOUR TARGET MARKET

You have to keep the proper perspective by continuously reevaluating the future of the music industry and knowing how to succeed in spite of the changes. Being mindful of the changing demographics and the aging population of the entire world (an entire world where people still "got to have it!") has to be a part of that perspective when planning your future business strategy and moving forward. Many record companies have aimed their marketing efforts primarily at the 13- to 24-year-old market, ignoring the older 35- to 55-year-old market, which grew up on and made the album/CD market flourish.

Time has proven that there will always be a market for boy bands like One Direction, The Wanted and 'tween sensations, Justin Beiber, Taylor Swift, Ariana Grande and Selena Gomez. But I believe it was the quest of Pop and American Idol founders, Simon Fuller and Cowell to find great undiscovered new talent that led to a burgeoning non-age restrictive 21st century Northern Soul movement of the late Amy Winehouse, Corinne Bailey Rae, Adele and Emile Sande . . . all artists with unique vocal and songwriting gifts. The breadth of sounds played on the radio and streamed on the Internet is truly astounding. From Lorde to

Michael Buble; Jay Z to Kendrick Lamar; Maroon Five to Imagine Dragons and Arcade Fire; Herbie Hancock to Esperanza Spalding; Greg Porter to the Robert Glasper Project; Country's Tim McGraw to Taylor Swift and Hunter Hayes, the variety of styles appreciated by vast markets of consumers is expanding. While labels had to reduce expenses and move to 360 degree deals to stay afloat during this seismic shift from the product to access-based model, tech giants Google, Apple and media moguls are investing in the record companies that can create powerful product in anticipation of a significant increase in the value of their assets before the end of the second decade of the 21st century.

An article in a recent edition of Billboard reported that Gospel Artist, Tamela Mann sold approximately 350,000 of the album, "Best Days" on Tillyman Records, the label she owns with her husband, actor and singer, David Mann. By owning their own label and having the records independently distributed the couple could reap up to $5.00 per album. At that rate, they may have earned over $1.75 M from the album sales spurned by the success of the album's first single "Take Me to the King." Now that's not to say that the entire million dollars is profit. But, because the label may not have a large staff or a number of other acts to invest in, it can retain a large percentage of the earnings. It is likely that other young, independent acts will follow suit once more artists understand what I've known for quite some time: that "you don't have to sell a million to make a million."

What does this spell? P-R-O-F-I-T for the independent record company. This is only bad news for artists looking for that major record label deal to get their career going. The reality is that the deal is more likely not going to be there. Why? Because if you aren't that one in a million act that can sell a million so the corporation can make millions, "foggedaboudit." So, what's the alternative? Are you out of the business before you even get started because you may not fit the profile or sound of that "one in a million act"? Not if you have and keep the proper perspective.

THE IMPORTANCE OF PROFESSIONAL ATTITUDE IN THE FUTURE

In the past, recording artists and other creative talents were not expected to display or possess the attributes of a professional beyond their performance in the studio or on a stage. However, many current performers not only possess the qualities of successful businesspersons, often bolstered by college degrees, but also publicly espouse the benefits to be attained by projecting a positive, professional attitude (Motown trained their artists to project such an attitude.) Their recognition of the potential for success from cross-media exploitation of their talents encourages them to approach each new opportunity as a step toward achieving goals their predecessors only dreamed of. Sean "Puffy" Combs (who, by the way, attended Howard University) has used his brand to launch restaurants, clothing, the number-one selling liquor, Ciroc Vodka and several other ventures. Similarly, Jay Z has used his celebrity to build his credibility with professional athletes. As a result, his Roc Nation Sports Agency has signed and negotiated several key athletes contracts, including a 10 year, $240M deal for baseball player, Robinson Cano. In addition to his Roc Nation label/management company and Sports Agency, Jay Z has also made the foray into restaurant/sports bar ownership with several 40/40 clubs across the U.S., and even the production of the Broadway play "Fela" with the help of another rapper/actor Will Smith and his wife, Jada Pinkett-Smith.

None of these ventures, which had to be accompanied by an investment of time and money, would have been possible without these stars professing and projecting a "Professional Attitude." Each of them recognized the opportunities available and capitalized on them with the assistance of competent and experienced professional advisers. In the future, more entertainers and their advisers will have to be well schooled (literally and figuratively) in several areas of expertise.

Besides grasping the fundamentals of developing and executing a business plan for each venture, one will need a variety of agreements detailing and clarifying each party's interest in each endeavor. As Judy Adams (widow of the late Blues/Rock & Roll singer Johnny Adams) said in the acceptance speech for her husband's posthumous Heritage Award from the R&B Foundation, "Don't walk, run, [to] and get a good attorney." The artists who get a good and experienced attorney, a competent accountant, and other knowledgeable business advisers will best display a professional attitude. A professional attitude will bring success and the success will be determined not only by the fame achieved, but also the fortune an artist (producer, artist, songwriter, etc.) is able to build for the future after acquiring such fame. I believe that success in the music business is not a myth or pipedream and it is still possible to build an empire based on available opportunities.

Artists like country superstar, George Strait has reached the pinnacle of success by featuring both new and veteran country artists like, Jason Aldean, Kenny Chesney, Eric Church, Ronnie Dunn, Vince Gill, Faith Hill, Alan Jackson, Miranda Lambert, Martina McBride, and Lee Ann Womack on his purported final "The Cowboy Rides Away Tour." R&B great Charlie Wilson has been featured on several tracks by rapper Kanye West and, as a result of pairing with great current R&B/Urban songwriters and producers, still hits the top of the Urban Contemporary charts with his solo releases; Both Tamar and Toni Braxton have turned a successful reality show, "Braxton Family Values" into a vehicle leading to number one singles for Tamar and a duet between Toni and Kenny "Babyface" Edmonds.

There is also the successful advent of artists of different genres who have recorded together in an effort to expand their fan base. You'll find that R. Kelly has teamed up with Lady Gaga for the duet, "Do What You Want," while "Blurred Lines" artist/songwriter, Robin Thicke, performed his hit on an awards show with members of the vintage group, Earth, Wind and Fire. Today, we also see many artists generally associated with one category of music recording material from other categories. They're "crossing over" to selling on different charts, recognizing that music is for the masses. Not only did former rock star Hootie and the Blowfish lead singer, Darius Rucker become a country music superstar but pop singers, Sheryl Crow and Lionel Richie also making the leap to country music. Yes! There are many and various ways to stay in business and the opportunities will be expanding even further in the future.

It is also important to know the market and that the styles of popular music are rapidly changing. Whereas in the first decade of the new millennium urban/rap artists were the big sellers, what were considered subgenres during that time—Pop, Country, and Electronic Dance Music (EDM)—are now the fastest-growing markets, with gospel music being introduced on the charts and in concert halls across the country in a whole new way.

POP

During the latter part of the last century and first few years of this century Pop music accounted for only 40–45% of the Billboard Mainstream Top 40, often squeezed off the chart by Country and R&B/Urban/Rap offerings. However, during the second decade of the new millennium the pure Pop sound has surged in this format. By 2012, almost 80% of the music on this Top 40 chart was considered pure Pop, representing the music of such artists as Lady Gaga, Katy Perry, Maroon 5 and others. This trend is still growing and is expected to continue as R&B/Urban acts like Usher, Trey Songz and country artists Lady Antebellum and Miley Cyrus and others release special singles solely targeted for the pop market. In addition, many hip-hop singles on this chart were replaced by more rhythmic pop by acts like Rihanna, Beyonce and Justin Timberlake. Hip hop is primarily represented in this format and the Billboard Hot 100 by artists like Macklemore and Ryan Lewis, Drake and guest-artist appearances on Pop hits like Eminem and Rihanna's "The Monster," T.I.'s rap on Robin Thicke's massive worldwide hit, "Blurred Lines," or Jay Z's similar contribution to

Justin Timberlake's "Suit and Tie," and Justin's reciprocal guest vocal on Jay Z's "Holy Grail."

ROCK

Rock music of the 1990s and early 21st century suffered the same fate as Pop, largely being eliminated from the playlists of Mainstream Top 40. The main exception was Grunge music in the early to mid-nineties. However, as of the time of this writing, sales of Rock music have surged with the genre accounting for 34% and 23% of total album and track sales, respectively. A number of both new and tested Rock artists have contributed to this increase. New artists Imagine Dreams, Fitz & the Tantrums and Vampire Weekend, join a cadre of established acts from a variety of styles, including The Fray, Arcade Fire, Mumford and Sons, The Killers, Arctic Monkeys, One Republic in creating a new demand for sales and streaming activity for a this historic genre.

ELECTRONIC DANCE MUSIC (EDM)

EDM has grown rapidly over the past few years, as the R&B/Soul/Disco beat of four on the floor has been resurrected for the dancing enjoyment of a whole new generation of partygoers. As the new millennium began, a new form of party, the rave, became just that, the rave in the entertainment industry. Largely fueled by the attendees use of the drug Estacy, raves became the place to experience not only the drug, but the effects the music can have on those who partake in the experience. Raves have since given way to both massive EDM festivals like Ultra Music, Electric Daisy, Winter Music Conference , Electric Zoo festivals and Las Vegas residencies by top EDM artists Kaskade, Avicii, David Guetta and others. The success of live promotion of this music has resulted in several EDM promotion companies being purchased by not only private investors, but large promoters like Live Nation and a venture named SFX. SFX, headed by Robert Sillerman, was the first company to consolidate the live promotion business in the 1990s by purchasing the businesses of most of the independent regional live promoters in the U.S. He sold the company in 2000 to the Clear Channel radio network that eventually spun the business off as Live Nation. Yep . . . the same Live Nation that dominates the current live performance scene. In 2012, Sillerman revived SFX with the intent of replicating the model he employed in the 90s, only this time consolidating the EDM market of independent promoters of festivals and events that herald this rapidly growing genre of music. His play was aided by an onslaught of success of EDM tracks appearing on Top 40 radio station playlists and dominating the Hot 100. While many speculate that EDM may suffer the same fate as Disco, dying a quick death in a backlash against the music spurned by a Chicago Rock music DJ in 1979, Sillerman insists that EDM is the "Sound of the Millienials" and has tremendous growth potential worldwide in both the live promotion, recorded music and sponsorship areas. Only time will tell!

COUNTRY

Country music has continued to be one of largest album selling markets. While coming in a close third to Rock and R&B, the number of certified gold and platinum albums top 20 of the Billboard Country Album charts routinely far exceeds those of the magazine's Top 200 Album and any other genre-specific chart. While live touring has always been a strength in the country market, the excitement of developing modern country artists that skew more to the Pop market, is leading to sold-out clubs, theaters and arenas across the U.S. However, the age-old controversy of old versus the new country sound is reaching a boiling point, as traditional artists favoring bands that both record and perform are being more vocal about their displeasure with modern country hit artists and songwriters dwelling on the all-to familiar lyrics dealing about trucks and beer and synthesized tracks dominating country radio playlists. Several new artists ascending to the top of the charts rely on this formula, much to the dismay of die-hard country loyalists. But, the development of artists like Hunter Hayes, Luke Bryan, Florida Georgia Line and others has expanded country's reach to the younger demographic that radio conglomerates crave and increases the sale of digital track downloads and streaming. It is a scene that is being repeated in other genres as well.

R&B

R&B music has, like country undergone significant change in respect to the old versus the modern sound of this important genre that was instrumental in the development of the current success of Urban and Pop music. The controversy hit a peak in the awarding of the 2013 American Music Award best R&B/Soul album to Justin Timberlake, who beat out the other nominees, Robin Thicke and Rihanna. As presenter comedian Sarah Silverman joked in introducing the nominees, "Wouldn't it be ironic if Rihanna is beat out for this award by a former Disney Mousekateer or the son of TV actor/personality Alan Thicke?" Not that any of the nominees were not worthy of the honor, but most traditional R&B fans were at a loss as to why great R&B artists like Charlie Wilson, Anthony Hamilton or Ledisi , were not in the running. In addition, the jazz roots of genre-bending artists like The Robert Glasper Project and Esperanza Spalding are pushing the boundaries of R&B in new directions, while at the same time maintaining traditional elements that appeal to both old and new audiences.

GOSPEL

Gospel music's sales market share has decreased recently but this category is proving to launch and develop the careers of several new artists like Lecrae, Tamela Mann, Marvin Sapp, Joshua Rodgers and others. Several of the major labels have purchased what used to be small, privately owned gospel labels, and directed this genre's sales beyond the traditional religious bookstore retailers. Many of these traditional Christian bookstores have evolved into "superstores," increasing their floor space and product selections to include DVDs and other products aimed at its target market. Although few gospel artists achieve gold or platinum certifications for their albums or singles, some, like Sapp and Mann sell several hundred thousand copies of albums. As the gospel market is still a viable album selling market, it will be even more important for musicians, singers, choir directors, and company owners to more fully understand the rights and obligations contained in contracts used primarily for rock, country, and R&B acts that sell significant numbers of albums. Contracts dealing with the relationship of gospel acts can be particularly complicated. Issues such as the size of the choir; who should or should not perform at recording sessions and live performances; what, if any, royalty should be paid to the choir members; as well as the effect of donations of members performances for the benefit of nonprofit corporations or church entities, are all important matters which should be agreed upon and reduced to writing to prevent disagreements should the act achieve the success of substantial record sales.

A proper perspective and professional attitude can assist artists, songwriters, producers, and record company executives who plan to stay in business. And as more artists branch out with their powerful product they'll recognize that what worked yesterday may not work the same way today to enable them to succeed in the future. But let's keep foremost in our minds that as professionals and creative people surviving in the record industry we've undertaken a broad endeavor and we have to recognize it is time—like no other—to Take Care of Your Music Business. And that's the gospel truth.

INDEX

accounting statements, 37, 95–106, 162–69, 200–203
across the board deal, 26–30
  "across the board" relationship, 27
  administering copyrights, 27, 28
  advances and royalties, 30
  agreements involved in, 29
  benefits of, 27–28
  conclusion concerning, 30
  conflict of interest, 26
  in contract language, 142–43, 150–51
  court challenges to, 29
  defined, 26
  diagram demonstrating, 29
  "double dipping," 26–27
  Exclusive Songwriter Contract, 142
  fiduciary duty awareness, 29–30
  naming operations, 29
  Personal Management Contract, 188, 189
  responsibilities in, 28
  revenue-sharing, 28
  risks/drawbacks of, 26–27, 28
  uses of, 26, 27
Adams, Judy, 227
Adele, 207
advances, 46–48
Agent & Manager magazine, 113
album prices, 99
American Federation of Musicians (AF of M), 59
American Federation of Television and Radio Artists/Screen Actors Guild (AFTRA/SAG), 59
Anthony, Marc, 207
Artist Empowerment Coalition, 39

ASCAP, 111, 164
Ashburn, Benjamin, 181
Ashford and Simpson, 133–34
audit/auditing, 57, 153

"Be Thankful for What You've Got," 163
Bennett, Tony, 196
Berger, Shelly, 33
Berk, Lawrence, 3
Berklee College of Music, 3
Beyonce, 32, 207
Bieber, Justin, 207
"Big 3" major labels, 13, 210
"Big 5" major labels, 12–13
"Big 6" major labels, 12, 210
Blackmon, Larry, 207
BMI, 111, 164
Bowie, David, 6
boy bands, 224
Bravo Merchandising, 35
Braxton, Tamar, 171
Braxton, Tamar and Toni, 227
"Braxton Family Values" series, 171, 227
Brown, Chris, 207
business model, new, 31–35
  360° deals, 32, 33, 35
  "across the board deals," 33
  ancillary income activities, 34–35
  Beyonce example, 32
  "the blessed trinity" of contracts, 33
  concept of an all-rights agreement, 32–33
  co-publishing agreement, 34
  development/singles' deal, 33–34
  label first and matching right provisions, 34

business model (*continued*)
  objections of artists, 34
  old business model, 32
  Published Price per Dealer (PPD), 34
  Robbie Williams, "all-rights" agreement of, 32
  royalties, 34
  superstar artists deals, 33
business structure of production companies, 18–25
  corporation, 22–24
    articles of incorporation, 22
    close corporations, 23–24
    corporate record book, 22
    defined, 22
    personal liability, 22
    subchapter S status tax designation, 23
    taxes, 23
    validity of, 22
  "de facto"entities, 18–19
  general partnership, 20–22
    defined, 20
    drawback to, 21–22
    personal liability, 21
    suitability of, 21
    taxes, 21
    written partnership agreement checklist, 20–21
    written vs. oral/implied agreement, 20
  limited liability company (LLC), 24–25
    benefits of, 24–25
    formation of, 25
    taxes, 25
  sole proprietorship, 19–20
    benefits of, 19
    "hired help" and, 19
    personal liability, 19
    risked in, 19
    taxes, 19–20

Caldwell, Hank, 217
California, 57, 176
Cameo group, 207, 217
"Cardiac Arrest," 207
Carlile, Brandi, 222–23

Carter, Troy, 171
Casablanca Records, 207
CD Baby's Derek Sivers, 7
Charles, Ray, 4
Chic, 114
Columbia Records, 4
Combs, Sean "Puffy ," 226
Commodores, The, 181
composition copyright earnings, 106, 111, 162
contemporary music education, 3
contracts and accounting statements, 36–37. See also Co-Publishing and Administration Contract; copyright earnings, statement and analysis of; Exclusive Recording Artist Contract; Exclusive Songwriter Contract; management earnings, statement and analysis of; Personal Management Contract; recording earnings, statement and analysis of
Cooke, Sam, 4
Coombs, Harry, 217
Co-Publishing and Administration Contract, 145–161
  administration fees, 152
  advances against royalties, 160
  analysis of agreement, 145–46
  assignment of contract, 159–160
  attorney-in-fact, 159
  attorneys' fees, 152
  communications, 158
  Compositions, 147
  copyright infringement, 155
  copyrights, 156
  indemnity, 156–57
  lyric sheets and biographical material, 155
  mechanical royalties, 152–53
  "Net Income," 151
  Participant agreement to granting rights to Company, 148–150
    right to collect income, 148
    right to exploit performances, 149
    right to issue mechanical reproduction licenses, 148–49

right to license and publish the compositions in printed music for, 149–150
right to license the compositions for synchronization, 149
right to manage, 148
right to substitute new titles or change selection lyrics, 150
Participant's portion, 147
Participants' right to inspect Company's books and records, 154
payments, 151–52
performing rights, 152
rights of the party and to the Compositions, 155–56
royalty payments, 153–54
shares, 151
sub-publishing contracts, 159
term of agreement, 150–51
third party offer, 157–58
third party right, 158
warranties or representations, 154
copyright earnings, statement and analysis of, 162–69
"Can't Get Enough" example, 163, 166, 167, 168 (table)
composition copyright earnings, 162
explanation of, 163
income streams, 164–69
   derivative right, 166–67
   mechanical right, 165–66
   performance right, 164
   synchronization right, 167–68
performance rights organizations, 164
copyright principles, 107–16
"bundle" copyright, 108
copyright claimant, 114
copyright registration, 108–9
the grand right, 116
importance of, 107
Motown Record Company example, 107–8
primary rights of copyright "bundle of rights," 109–16
   derivative right, 113–16
   mechanical right, 109–11
   synchronization right, 112–13

the print right, 116
sampling, 113–16
corporation, 22–24
Country music, 230–31
Crow, Sheryl, 227

Daniels, George, 11
Davis, Clive, 217
The Decade, 206
Devaughn, William, 163
digital age, the evolving, 210–14
   albums, 211
   business model change, 211
   Future of Music Coalition (FMC), 212
   The Future of Music (Kusek and Leonhard), 212
   Internet marketing, 212
   live performance, growth of, 212
   "music like water" model, 212
   P2P file sharing, 210
   piracy, 210
   record sales, 210–11
   recording industry consolidation, 210
   reduced earnings, 211
   revenue sharing, 213
   singles market, 211
   synchronization, 211–12
Dion, Celine, 177
Disco music, 4
Dole, Bob, 124
"double dipping," 26–27, 159
Dr. Dre, 170
Drake, 170

Earth, Wind and Fire, 227
eCO form, 114
eCO form of copyright registration, 114
Edwards, Bernard, 114
Electronic Dance Music (EDM), 221–22, 229–230
EMI, 32, 210
Eminem, 49
entrepreneurialism, 4
Eventful.com, 212
Exclusive Recording Artist Contract, 38–94
   360° (All-rights) provision, 78–81

Exclusive Recording Artist Contract
  (*continued*)
 advances, 46–48
 approvals, 91–92
 assignment, 77
 California law and, 57
 co-publishing, 86–90
 definitions, 65–70
 distribution agreement, 90–91
 failure of performance, 78
 grant of rights, 48–51
 legal and equitable relief, 76–77
 mechanical licenses, 73–76
 miscellaneous, 92–94
 name and likeness; merchandising: touring: additional activities, 78–84
 notices, 77–78
 recording commitment, 42–44
 recording costs, 45–46
 recording procedure, 44–45
 recording services, 42
 royalties, 51–55
 royalty accountings, 55–59
 suspension and termination, 70–73
 term or length of time, 38–41
 videos, 84–86
 warranties, representations, restrictions and indemnities, 59–65
Exclusive Songwriter Contract, 117–144
 accounting, 130–32
 across the board deal, 142
 actions, 136–37
 analysis of agreement, 117–18
 assignment, 140
 collaboration, 132
 compensation/royalties, 126–130
 co-ownership and administration, 142
 definitions, 140
 employment, 118
 entire agreement, 139
 exclusivity, 124
 grant of rights, 119–124
 heading, 141–42
 indemnity, 137–38
 inducement, 143
 modification, waiver, invalidity, and controlling law, 139–140
 notices, 138–39
 other arrangements, 142–43
 power of attorney, 125–26
 recoupment, 143
 separate agreements, 132–33
 suspension and termination, 141
 term, 118–19
 unique services, 135–36
 warranties, representations, covenants and agreements, 124–25
 writer's services, 133–35

Facebook, 7
fiduciary duty, 29–30
Fray, The, xv
Frontline Management, 35
Future of Music Coalition (FMC), 212
The Future of Music (Kusek and Leonhard), 212

Gaye, Marvin, 218
general partnership, 20–22
Gordy, Berry, 4, 108, 220
Gospel music, 231–32
Grunge music, 229

Hamilton, Anthony, 231
Hank Caldwell, 217
Hayes, Isaac, 124
Herbert, Vincent, 171
Hines, Eddie, 206
Hip hop, 228
Houston, Whitney, 170

The Illusions, 205
Imagine Dragons, 207
information, incorporating the, 214–15
 attorney or accountant fees, 214
 business plan, 215
 contracts, 215
 diversifying income, 215
 education, 215
International Talent Management, Inc., 33
Internet music streaming, 6–7, 102–6, 218, 219
iRadio, 212
iTunes, 6

Jackson, Curtis (50 Cent), 182
Jackson, Sandra, 12
Jay Z, 226
Jewel, 220
Jobete affiliate, 133
Jobs, Steve, 6

Kellogg, Clark, 14
Kelly, R., 227
Kickstarter, 7
King, Joe, xv (image)
Kusek, Dave, 212

Lady Gaga, 170, 227
Ledisi, 231
Leonhard, Gerd, 212
Levert, Gerald, 217
limited liability company (LLC), 24–25
Live Nation, 32, 221–22, 230
live performance, 204–9
   Amanda Palmer example, 209
   choreographic performers, 207
   fan relationship and, 209
   growth of live performance market, 204
   importance of, 204, 207
   international festivals, 204
   the "It" theory, 205–9
      having "It," 205
      making "It," 206–7
      working "It," 205–6
   musicianship and, 207
   notable performers, 207
   O'Jays example, 204–5
   vs. recording, 207–8
Lopez, Jennifer, 207
"Love to Love You Baby," 207

management earnings, statement and analysis of, 200–203
   endorsements, 201–2
   live performances, 201
   movie roles, 202–3
   third-party producer activities, 201
Mann, Tamela and David, 225
Mayfield, Curtis, 218
mechanical right, 109–11
mergers and acquisitions of major labels, 13

Michelle, Chrisette, 11
Motown Record Company, 4, 107
Motown-the Musical, 220
MP-3 technology, 5
MTV, 5
music business and the future, 216–232
   Brandi Carlile example, 222–23
   Broadway production, 220
   consolidation, 222–24
      artists concerns about, 222
      downsizing and, 223
      Electronic Dance Music (EDM) market, 221–22
      high overhead and, 223–24
      Live Nation, 221–22
      Newsweek magazine on, 222
      UMG and EMI consolidation, 223
      Universal Music Group, 223
   costs of recording, 221
   Country music, 230–31
      expansion of, 231
      live performance, 230
      notable performers, 231
      old versus new country sound, 230–31
   Electronic Dance Music (EDM), 221–22, 229–230
   expansion of the entertainment business, 218–19
   Gospel music, 231–32
      Christian bookstores and, 232
      contract dealing with, 232
      major labels and, 232
      notable performers, 231, 232
   Hip hop, 228
   Internet record streaming, 218, 219
   Live Nation, 230
   Pop music, 228–29
      construction of, 228
      notable performers, 228–29
   powerful product and the future, 219–221
   professional attitude, importance of, 226–28
      Charlie Wilson, 227
      Darius Rucker, 228
      Earth, Wind and Fire, 227
      George Strait, 227

music business and the future (*continued*)
  Jay Z, 226
  Judy Adams, 227
  R. Kelly/Lady Gaga, 227
  Robin Thicke, 227
  Sean "Puffy" Combs, 226
  Tamar and Toni Braxton, 227
 proper perspective for the future, 221–24
 R&B music, 231
  notable performance, 231
  old versus the modern sound of, 231
 reevaluation, 224
 Rock music, 229
  contraction of, 229
  Grunge music, 229
  notable performers, 229
 synthesized sound, backlash against, 221
 target market, 224–25
  boy bands, 224
  breadth of, 224–25
  Northern Soul movement, 224
 technological announcements, 220–21
music industry, growth and development of, 1–7
 annual revenue growth of records (1954–58), 4
 Berklee College of Music, 3
 compact displayer, 4–5
 contemporary music education, 3
 Disco music, 4
 downsizing, 1
 entrepreneurialism, 4
 Internet sharing (P2P file sharing), 5
 Internet streaming services, 6–7
 iTunes, 6
 major labels, tactics of, 5
 MP-3 technology, 5
 music videos, 5
 Napster, 5
 new business models, 1
 paradigm shift, 1
 radio programming, 3
 record company earnings (1999– 2012), 6
 records, 3
 Rock and Roll, 3
 royalty rates, 6
 sale of records, 4
 sheet music business, 2
 social networking, 7
 SONY Walkman, 4
 Spotify, 6
 technological innovation, 1–4
 television, 3
 Web sites with ancillary services and products, 7
 YouTube, 6
music production company, 8–9
 composition of, 8
 defined, 8
 earlier, 8–9
 growth of, 9–10
 independent production companies, 9
 as "subcontractors," 8
Myspace, 7

Napster, 5, 211
Network Records, 217
The New Decade, 217
New York, 176
The New York City Players, 217
Newsweek magazine, 222
N'Syn, 172

O'Jays, The, 204–5, 207, 208, 216–17

P Diddy, 170
P2P file sharing, 5, 32, 102, 210, 211
Pace, Harry, 2
Palmer, Amanda, 209
Pandora, 212
performance rights organizations, 164
Perry, Katy, 207
Personal Management Contract, 170–199
 across the board deal, 188, 189
 analysis of agreement, 172–73
 as an arm's length transaction, 198–99
 assignment, 191, 193–94
 attorney-in-fact, 177–79
 breach by artist, 190

INDEX 239

breach of contract/act of omission, 187–88
California talent agent laws, 176
commissions, 188–89
compensation, 180–85
credit, 194
crossover talent, 170
Curtis Jackson (50 Cent) endorsement example, 182
employment and manager, 175–76
engagement of manager, 173–74
exclusivity, 173–74, 179–180
expenses, 185–86
female artist, 198
"good faith opinion," 193
groups provision, 196–98
importance of manager, 170–71
life insurance provision, 195–96
manager and artist relationship, 187
manager's commissions, 172
manager's outlook, 171
managing with a "long view," 171
New York talent agent laws, 176
non-revocable provision, 194
ownership, 195
payment, 178–79, 193
personal management services agreement, 174–75
power of attorney, 176–79
Tamar Braxton example, 171
Philadelphia International Records label, 217
Pit Bull, 207
Pop music, 228–29
Porter, Gregory, 207
powerful product, 11–12, 219–221
PPD (published price to dealer), 34, 51, 53, 99–100
Prince, 39, 61

Queen Latifah, 220

R&B music, 231
radio programming, 3
Rae, Corinne Bailey, 224
"Rappers Delight," 114
Rdio, 212

"reasonable and promising" contract terms, 175
record company earnings (1999–2012), 6
recording earnings, statement and analysis of, 95–106
    first assumption, 96–97
    second assumption in, 96–97
    third assumption in, 97
    four assumption in, 98
    album prices, 99
    "all-in" designation of a fund or royalty, 96
    "all-in recording fund" type of agreement, 96, 97, 98
    "all-in royalty," 97
    assumptions in statement of recording earnings, 96–98
    digital download third-party use, 102
    PPD (published price to dealer), 99–100
    "recording budget," 96
    royalties, 104
    royalties from sales of albums and singles, 98–99 (table)
    royalties from third party uses, 100–101
    sample royalty statement, 105 (table)
    sampling, 102
    SoundExchange, 104
    streaming, 102–6
    suggested retail list price (SRLP), 99
    synchronization uses, 101
Recording Industry Association of America (RIAA), 104
Rhapsody, 212
Richie, Lionel, 227
Rihanna, 231
Roc Nation Sports Agency, 226
Rodgers, Niles, 114
Rolling Stones, 207
royalties, 34
    cross-collateralization, 160
    digital performance, 104
    in Exclusive Recording Artist Contract, 51–59
    mechanical, 152–54
    reduction of, 6

royalties (*continued*)
  from sales of albums and singles, 98–99 (table)
  sample royalty statement, 105 (table)
  from third party uses, 100–101
Rucker, Darius, 227
Ruffin, David, 33, 205

Sagan, Carl, 1
sampling
  copyright claimant, 114
  defined, 102
  derivative rights, 114
  eCO form of copyright registration, 114
  license or clearance agreemen, 115
  monetary effect of using, 115
  PA type of copyright registration, 114
  sample clearance "houses," 115–16
  SR form of copyright registration, 114
  technical definition of, 113
  true case of sampling, 114–15
  warning about, 115
Sande, Adele and Emile, 224
Santana, 177
SESAC, 87, 111, 128, 164
Shapiro, Louis, 2
Shapiro & Bernstein, 2
sheet music business, 2
Shorter, Wayne, 207
Sillerman, Robert, 230
Silverman, Sarah, 231
Sinatra, Frank, 4
singles market, 51
Slade, Isaac, xv
sole proprietorship, 18–20
Sonicbids, 212
Sonicbid's Panos Panay, 7
SONY, 5
SONY Music Entertainment, 13
SONY Walkman, 4
SONY/ATV, 210
SoundCloud, 7
SoundExchange, 104
Spears, Britney, 177
Spotify, 6, 212

Strait, George, 227
streaming, 218
  ad supported, 1
  exposure of artists, 28
  powerful product and, 219
  recording earnings, 102–3, 104
  services, 6, 212
  third-party use, 101
subchapter S status tax designation, 23
suggested retail list price (SRLP), 99
Summer, Donna, 207
synchronization
  rights, 112–13, 167–68
  uses, 101, 128, 149, 211

taxes, 19–20, 21, 23–24
television, 3
Thicke, Robin, 227, 231
The Three Big P's, 10–17
  big money, lure of, 13–14
  memories and emotion, 12
  powerful product, 11–12
  professional attitude, 16–17
  proper perspective, 12–16
    external factor, 12
    internal component, 13
    "When a Million Dollars Ain't a Million Bucks" theory, 13–16
Timberlake, Justin, 172, 207, 231
TIN (tax identification number), 21
Topspin, 7
TuneCore, 7
Twitter, 7
Tyner, McCoy, 207

U2, 207
UMG and EMI consolidation, 223
Underwood, Carrie, 170
Universal Music Group, 13, 34–35, 49, 210, 223
Universal Music's Pressplay, 6
Usher, 207

Warner Bros. Records, 39
Warner Music Group, 13
Web sites with ancillary services and products, 7

Welsh, Dave, xv (image)
"When a Million Dollars Ain't a Million Bucks" theory, 13–16
Williams, Robbie, 32
Wilson, Charlie, 227, 231
Winehouse, Amy, 224

Withers, Bill, 113
Wonder, Stevie, 218
Wysocki, Ben, xv (image)

YouTube, 6, 7, 212

BIO

John P. Kellogg, Esq. is Assistant Chair of Music Business Management at Berklee College of Music in Boston, Massachusetts and an entertainment lawyer. A former vocalist with the group Cameo, he has represented Levert, The O'Jays, Eddie Levert, Sr., LSG, Stat Quo of Shady/Aftermath Records, G-Dep of Bad Boy Records and the late R&B artist Gerald Levert. His first book, Take Care of Your Music Business, The Legal and Business Aspects You Need to Know to Grow in the Music Industry has been sold world-wide. Also the author of numerous legal articles and editorials, John has been profiled in *Billboard*, *Ebony*, and *Jet* magazines and named to *Ebony* magazine's Power 150 list of African-American Organization Leaders. Serving his seventh year and also as past president, he is seated on the Board of Directors of the Music and Entertainment Industry Educators Association. An inductee into the Black Entertainment and Sports Lawyer's Association Hall of Fame, he provides radio commentary on Power 620 AM, serves as a talent judge on the Emmy-award winning Community Auditions and reports about music industry issues on a number of radio, television, and online stations. His current client list includes saxophonist Walter Beasley, Internet sensation Emily Luther, composer Bill Banfield, gospel artist Jason Champion, and Eddie Levert of The O'Jays. He received a Bachelor of Arts Degree in Political Science, a Master of Science Degree in Television and Radio at Syracuse University and the Newhouse School of Communication and his Juris Doctor at Case Western Reserve University School of Law.

Attorney Kellogg is licensed to practice in the states of New York and Ohio.

For additional information about the author, please visit www.kellogglaw.com

Legal Articles, Editorials, and Commentaries by John P. Kellogg

The Urbanization of the Billboard Charts: How Soundscan Changed the Game

Free the Music! An Examination of the Section 115 Music Reform Act of 2006

Remembering Gerald Levert

Do Recording Artists Deserve a Greater Share of Revenue in the Emerging Digital Age?

Royalty Audit Takes Effect in California

An Awakened Sleeping Giant Supports Legislative Initiatives to Reform the Exclusive Recording Artist Agreement

Adult R&B: Keep It Real

Adult R&B: Just the Same Old Oldies

Livin' the 'Singles' Life

Contractual Concerns for Rhythm & Rap Music Artists in the Ever Expanding "Hood"

Bankruptcy and the Exclusive Recording Agreement

Recording Artist Remember . . . Your Talent Is the Power

Rap Artist Managers Beware: Sampling Can Be Hazardous to Your Financial Health

Rappers Beware! Sampling Can Be Hazardous to Your Financial Health

Copyrights: A Most Valuable Asset

Lawmakers of the 20th Century

Bankruptcy: A System of Justice Designed to Renew and Restore

Pursuing Justice for All

Family Business Is Strictly Business

For additional information on these and other articles by the author, please visit www.kellogglaw.com